Calling Texas Home

A Lively Look at What It Means to Be a Texan

WELLS TEAGUE

Foreword by David L. Lindsey

WILDCAT CANYON PRESS
A Division of Circulus Publishing Group, Inc.
Berkeley, California

Publisher: Tamara Traeder
Editorial Director: Roy M. Carlisle
Marketing Director: Carol Brown
Managing Editor: Leyza Yardley
Production Coordinator: Larissa Berry
Copyeditor: Jean Blomquist
Cover Design: Gordon Chun Design
Interior Design and Typesetting: Margaret Copeland/Terragraphics
Typographic Specifications: Text in Century Old Style 10/15, headings in Giddyup and
Century Old Style Bold.

Printed in Canada

Library of Congress Cataloging-in-Publication Data
Teague, Wells,
    Calling Texas home : a lively look at what it means to be a Texan / by Wells Teague.
      p. cm — (Calling it home series)
    ISBN 1-885171-38-2 (alk. paper)
    1. Texas—Social life and customs—Miscellanea. 2. Texas—History—Miscellanea.
    I. Title. II. Series.

F386.6 .T4 2000
976.4—dc21   00-042278

Distributed to the trade by Publishers Group West

10 9 8 7 6 5 4 3 2   01 02 03 04 05

Contents

Acknowledgments

My thanks go first of all to Dana Whitney Gard, who suggested to Roy Carlisle that I should write *Calling Texas Home*. I knew immediately it was a subject already mine, but Roy had no way to know. So thanks, Roy, for your trust (and probably prayers). Staff members of the Texas Historical Commission's library, fittingly located in the wonderful Gethsemane Church—whose stone was hauled by wheelbarrow from a burned Texas state capitol building more than a hundred years ago—provided help with research questions.

The book wouldn't have come about without my sister, Doris Durrett of Abernathy, who wrote pieces, and talked to her friends, and made Ern tell his story. You'll see her touches throughout the book.

In these pages you will encounter Bill Nance, a dyed-in-the wool Texan if there ever was one, who goes public with the hardest subject a Texas coach ever has to face—a losing season. But more, Bill contributed his time and efforts throughout the writing and gathering process.

Alvaro Guevara was my Spanish language expert. Now, Al, you will always be linked with the Texas state bird, *el cincsonctle*, the mockingbird.

And for many, there is just thanks. You each know what for: Daryl Henderson Brand, Tomás Villarreal, Betty Fuston, Ellen Bishop, Beth Ann Ball, Charlotte Shultz, Anne Neel, Roman Echezaretta; L.T. Bailey; Kathy Allen; Pernicia and Glynn Durrett, Horace and Ellen Morgan; and of Mertzon, Rena Thorp. For John Smith, thanks for the encouragement.

I owe thanks of a different sort to many of my Texans who are no longer living—my father and mother who told me old stories, and my mother's brother, Robert Caruthers, who, in my personal pantheon ranks approximately with Socrates. And my brother, Lewis Dale Teague, who didn't quite make it long enough to receive his copy. Long ago in Sweetwater there was the first of my many dedicated teachers who made me want to read—Mrs. Ardis Gaither—and

v

in Lubbock, my greatest mentor, Charles Lawrie. Charles knew everything about opera, literature, maps, and Carl Jung, and had a good start on Texas, although he was born in Wisconsin, like a lot of good Texans. He was also my best man.

They are all here, if not on stage then in the wings, with all thumbs up.

★ ★

For Karon

and

Heather, Jonathan, and Summer

"Texas, Margaret, Texas!"

Sam Houston's last words, to his wife

Foreword

The words "Texas" and "big" have been used so often in the same sentence that you could publish a book of a generous size comprised solely of sentences containing those words. And you could publish a second volume of similar size comprised of sentences in which "Texas" and "myth" have been used together. But these two small words, which conjure up such grand imagery, have tended to reduce the "idea" of Texas to an oversimplified, one-dimensional caricature, a bumper-sticker depiction of one of the nation's most complex states.

Many have argued that homogeneity is in our national destiny, that eventually everywhere will be like everywhere else as the powers of commerce try to remake us all in the same image so they can sell all of us the same products in the same packages at the same prices. Some have argued, too, that America's regionalism is threatened by our national media encouraging us to wear the same brand-name clothes, drive the same kind of vehicles, see the same movies, and watch the same television sitcoms.

But oversimplified ideas and neat theories of creeping sameness will eventually have to confront the reality of an irrepressible stubbornness in the American spirit, a mulish individuality that refuses to be categorized and confounds all predictions. This spirit of irascible orneriness is found in superabundance in Texas, and all the clichés in the world can't protect the traveler from encountering it in every corner of the state, from the Piney Woods to the Big Bend, from the Panhandle to the Valley. Texas is *suis generis* . . . one of a kind, and it revels in its eccentricities. That's one of the fine things about the state, it has a keen appreciation of its own originality . . . and it cultivates it with pride.

Those of us who were born in Texas and have never lived anywhere else (and have never wanted to live anywhere else), hardly feel deprived of the variety that is proverbially said to be the spice of life. Every little town, and there

are thousands of them scattered across the state like stars in the Milky Way, is its own microcosm. All of life is there, recast in the image of local actors. I have known any number of Falstaffs in the towns where I rambled in my youth, and not a few Hamlets, too, strutting their stuff upon the stage and casting a suspicious eye upon the local shenanigans.

Calling Texas Home is your introduction to the nation of Texas. Enjoy the book and enjoy the state. Don't analyze it or try to figure it out. It can't be done. Just relish the variety of it and get into the spirit of a state with a spirit all its own. Contrary to some opinions, you don't have to be born in Texas to call it home. No, sir, it's a welcoming state. But it does help if you can view the world from a slightly different angle than most people. If you can't do that at first, don't worry about it. You'll get the hang of it, and before you know it you'll be *Calling Texas Home* too.

—David L. Lindsey, *Austin*

Sixty-Five Million Years B.C.

A Giant Flying Pterosaur, *Quetzalcoatlus sevenfortysevenii*[1] (known to his neighbors as the Pa-**terror**-saur next door), is just soaring along, about a thousand feet up, enjoying the updrafts. Quetzal is fresh from a morning wading in a freshwater pond snacking on oh, clams, mussels, some things unidentifiable. Suddenly he doesn't feel so hot. Chills in the midsection. Smoke in his cockpit. Mayday! Flaps his twenty-foot wings for the last time; nosedives into the ooze. *Zzzz oooo mmmm* **smunkt!**

Sixty-five million years later the ooze has turned to stone. The site is now known as Big Bend. Specialists in paleoreptilian aeronautics dig up Quetzal's remains. *Hmmm. This is one **big** dude.* They examine his *levelizer stabilisimus*, measure his fractured *fractumus*, and peer into the cavities of his helium-filled vertebrae. *This is the **biggest** pterosaur we have **ever** seen. Wooee! Look at them flappin' wing bones!*

The bones stir and the scientists jump back. Quetzal shakes the dust off his skull, looks around, **brightens up,** utters his now famous cry:

YeeeeeeHaaa! I'm in *Texas*!

[1] The real Texas pterosaur was *Quetzalcoatlus northropi,* found in 1971 by Doug Lawson, a student of Texas Memorial Museum's Wann Lanston, Jr. With a wingspan up to fifty feet, it is the largest flying animal yet discovered. Its fossilized cry has not yet been found.

Where We Came From

Now pay attention. What comes next is not a history lesson. Say it ten times: *This is* not *a history lesson*. I wrote it down so I could figure out how Texas got here, and you can read it if you want to.

Piñeda

In 1519 the Spanish sea captain **Alonzo Álvarez de Piñeda** mapped the coast of the Gulf of Mexico from Florida to Veracruz looking for a passage to India. He produced a remarkably accurate drawing—which still exists—including the area now known as the Texas Gulf Coast. Piñeda and his crew were the first Europeans to gaze upon the shores of Texas. But true settlement was a long time coming. Portugal and Spain, the two most powerful nations in the world at the time Columbus discovered you-know-what, had divided up the spoils in 1494 through the Treaty of Tordesillos. The division line was called the *Line of Tordesillos.* In the New World it clipped the eastern edge of South America, giving Portugal only Brazil. Spain got the rest, which of course included the land that would be Texas and the sea that would be the Gulf of Mexico. So, for a hundred and fifty years the Spaniards had plenty of chances to secure the new lands. In 1495, by establishing technical training schools for navigators, Spain began to develop pilots who could, by a mathematical system called "dead reckoning," record with excellent accuracy the whereabouts of their ships relative

to a starting point. They could draw pretty good maps too. They established such clever procedures as collecting sediment from anchorage sites and sending descriptions of the sediment back home with its place of origin marked on a map. That way, the king's sediment technicians could compare it with earlier samples of the bottom stuff and figure out where the new sample had come from. This was the world's first **Dirt Database** and the beginning of Texas's involvement with high technology.

Anyway, the **Spaniards were really into sailing.** They built and outfitted ships, manned them with sailors, pilots, tradesmen, and priests; piled on enormous loads of armor, weapons, tools, skiffs, pottery, any kind of food lacking vitamin C, horses, cattle, goats, and sheep; and very important, thick *fictiones* about Knight Errantry. The Spanish *escribanos* entered the final ship's inventory in their ledgers that were the size of small houses. Then they sheathed their quill pens and walked outside with everyone else to await wind. The launch was always a festive occasion, especially when a flotilla of a half dozen or so ships was trying to leave. When the wind grew favorable, the *conquistadores* (conquerors) climbed aboard, visions of the Seven Golden Cities jingling in their heads. The low-riding, creaking, already smelly wooden ships, each about the size of a 1959 Cadillac Sedan de Ville, wallowed toward the New World.

So it was one of these Spaniards and his shipmates who first mapped the crescent-shaped coast of the Gulf of Mexico from Florida to Vera Cruz. Earlier that year (we're still in 1519), one of Piñeda's countrymen, **Hernán Cortés, founded Veracruz, took Tenochtitlan from the Aztecs, and renamed it Mexico City.** All in a day's work for a Spanish *conquistador*, for whom *The Power of Positive Thinking* had been a required text back at sailing school.

Cabeza de Vaca

The first ship wreck (actually a raft wreck) that made a difference in getting the Texas country noticed began with the 1532 Pánfilo de Narváez expedition with Alvar Núñez on board. Núñez would become famous as Cabeza de Vaca, which means "head of a cow." Captain Narváez put himself and his party ashore in Florida and sent his ships to reconnoiter the coast. *The ships never returned.* Coffee break must have been long overdue. Narváez and his men put to sea on rafts, hoping to float to Veracruz on the opposite shore of the Gulf of Mexico, but (of course) they piled up on the Texas coast. It was cold that winter on the coast. Fifteen out of eighty men survived until spring. Cabeza de Vaca, whose grandfather must have been a camel, walked through Texas, into northern Mexico, and south to Mexico City, where he reported his adventures to Cortés. His sojourn lasted eight years, and little of it was pleasant. But he said the **Indians talked about golden cities.** And you know what rumors of gold do to the human heart. After subsisting on pecans and cactus fruit for eight years, Cabeza didn't want to go back, even to look for golden cities.

Coronado

In 1540 the socially prominent governor of Nueva Gallicia in western Mexico **gets his chance** to find the golden cities. Francisco Vasquez de Coronado's party consists of a dust-raising crowd of 1,000 men, 1,500 horses and mules, a good-sized larder-on-the-hoof, and two ships sent up the west coast of Mexico for support. (Cabeza de Vaca could have told Coronado when he would see these ships again.) For two years this ensemble disturbed the future American Southwest, including the Palo Duro Canyon in the northern Panhandle of Texas. They alienated the natives, scattered horses and cattle, and created for

themselves an entire page in Texas history schoolbooks 450 years later. But of gold, they heard only rumors. In 1542 Coronado returned to Mexico to defend himself on charges of mishandling the expedition and forgetting to govern Nueva Gallicia.

Treasure Ships

After gathering up Montezuma's gold, Cortés turned his attention to other riches of the Mexican countryside. Soon the Spaniards began sending ships laden with Mexican silver back to Spain. These treasure ships followed the wind and the Caribbean Current in a clockwise motion through the Gulf. They entered it on the south end of Cuba through the Yucatán Channel, loaded the silver at Veracruz, sailed north and east along the coast, and left the Gulf on the north end of Cuba through the Straits of Florida and thus into the Atlantic. This route brought the convoys close against the barrier islands of Texas, where, with satisfying regularity, they wrecked. To wit: in the fall of 1553 a convoy of twenty ships carrying 2,000 passengers sails out of Veracruz. At least three ships break up on Padre Island. **The passengers and crew clamber out on the sand and find themselves facing bands of cannibalistic Karankawa Indians, who are making a mysterious smacking noise.** One of those they don't eat, Frey Marcos de Medina, walks 400 miles to Tampico and makes his report: "Looks like we need to advise the king to put more money into weather radar and bottom planking," he probably said, while bathing his feet. He, like Cabeza de Vaca, does not request to be returned to Texas immediately.

And the authorities don't have the nerve to advise the king on anything. Progress is stalled. The Karankawas, after looking hopefully to the Gulf for a few days, return to their regular diet of crustaceans, bugs, and roots. The next year, a storm drives three more Spanish treasure ships ashore on Padre Island. And so it goes for a couple of centuries.

The Woman in Blue

Maria Agreda (1602–65) of Castile, Spain, was obviously a Texan, though she never physically visited here. **She had visions** in which she walked the lands of Texas saving the souls of Indians. Simultaneously, Spanish missionaries in Texas were getting reports from the Indians of a European maiden, the Woman in Blue, who had visited them, urging them to seek salvation. Maria became famous throughout Europe.

Here First

Texas has one of the nation's largest populations of Native Americans. More than 70,000 American Indians live in Texas—mostly in urban areas, with the highest concentration in Dallas and Fort Worth. These folks can vote in regular local, state, and federal elections, and also in the elections held in their Indian nation. **There are three reservations in the state,** each with a population of around 500. The Tigua reservation is on the east side of El Paso; the Kickapoo reservation is located southeast of Eagle Pass (where many of the tribal members still live in their traditional houses made out of river cane); and the Alabama and Coushatta reservation is near Livingston, in East Texas. This latter spot is a top tourist attraction. Their radio station broadcasts in the Coushatta language for part of the day.

The site of the last permanent settlement in East Texas of the Caddo Indians has recently been found in Marion County. It is named Timber Hill, which in Caddo is *Shahshildahnee*. The Caddoes left it more than 100 years ago.

The Tigua tribe has voted on its new governor by a show of hands every New Year's Eve since before 1700. For the year 2000 the tribe selected Albert Alvidrez, who at twenty-seven is the youngest governor in Tigua history.

Most people who read about the frontier days in Texas think there were only a couple of Native American groups in Texas, the Comanches and Kiowas. Not only were there many groups, but they were highly mobile. They followed food sources and traveled long distances for supplies such as salt and flint. The Spanish encountered many of these traveling bands. **Here are 396 Native American tribes** reported in Texas by non-Indians between 1528 and 1750. I've listed them in the order they were "discovered." Please be able to recite them in alphabetical order at the beginning of our next page. Now don't get upset. The number of tribes figures out to only 1.559 per county. Also, I've had them printed in a very small font. If you can't read the letters, you don't have to do the test.

Atayo, Coaque, Doguene, Han, Maliacone, Quevene, Quitole, Teya, Caddo, Hacanac, Kadodacho, Lacane, Jumano, Tanpachoa, Tepelguan, Escanjaque, Manso, Cacaxtle, Bobole, Muruam, Manos Colorados, Ocana, Quarai, Cocoma, Pachaque, Pataguo, Pinanaca, Bibit, Ervipame, Espopolame, Gueiquesale, Hape, Heniocane, Hume, Pinanca, Taimamar, Yorica, Pinto, Piro, Tiguex, Tigua, Penunde, Quide, Quioborique, Quitaca, Tohaha, Unojita, Utaca, Agua Sucia, Arihuman, Bean, Borobama, Caimane, Come Comocara, Flechas Feas, Geobari, Janaque, Los Surdos, Mana, Mano, Miembros Largos, Muele, Neuz, Obori, Pescado, Tishim, Tixemu, Toapa, Toapare, Pamorano, Aba, Abau, Achubale, Aguioa, Aieli, Anchimo, Arcos Tuertos, Asen Arcos, Bajunero, Beitonijure, Bobida, Caula, Colabrote, Conchamucha, Cujaco, Cujalo, Cunqueback, Detobiti, Diju, Echancote, Flechas Chiquitas, Hanasine, Henehi, Hinsa, Huane, Huicasique, Inhame, Isucho, Jedionda, Novrach, Ororoso, Pagaiam, Paiabuna, Patzau, Pojue, Pucha, Pucham, Puguahiane, Pulcha, Quicuchabe,

Quisaba, Quitaca, Siacucha, Suajo, Suma, Teanda, Tojuma, Torgme, Unojita, Ylame, Yoyehi, Nabedache, Ahehouen, Anachorema, Annaho, Palaquesson, Quara, Taraha, Daquio, Datcho, Erigoanna, Haque, Hianagouy, Hiantatsi, Kabaye, Keremen, Korona, Mayeye, Meracouman, Nadamin, Ointemarhen, Omenaosse, Petao, Spichehat, Caiaban, Cannaha, Cannahio, Cantey, Cassia, Erigoanna, Kannehouan, Kanohatino, Neche, Pamoque, Panequo, Quinet, Quiouaha, Tahiannihouq, Tchanhié, Nabiri, Emet, Mescale, Quem, Telamene, Samampac, Sampanal, Cabia, Ebahamo, Manam, Manico, Naaman, Nacau, Paac, Paachique, Pachal, Pacuache, Paguan, Panasiu, Papanac, Pastaloca, Payaya, Payuguan, Pitahay, Pulacuam, Semonan, Causquetebano, Toaa, Too, Emet, Manico, Paachique, Pasteal, Patague, Patzau, Putayy, Sana, Tecahuiste, Tojo, Paouite, Anao, Bata, Caai, Cagaya, Canabatinu, Canonioiba, Canonizochitoui, Canu, Caquixadaquix, Casiba, Cataqueza, Caxo, Caynaaya, Datana, Dico, Guasa, Odoesmade, Pacpul, Quibaga, Quiguaya, Quiutcauaha, Sana, Sico Teniba, Tobo, Vidix, Vinta, Xanna, Zauanito, Zonomi, Ocana, Paac, Pastaloca, Pitahay, Vanca, Mepayaya, Nabeyxa, Arcos Buenos, Arcos Pordidos, Arcos Tirados, Borrado, Cabellos Blancos, Cabeza, Canaq, Casas, Moradas, Colas Largas, Come Cibolas, Conejo, Cruiamo, Dientes Alazanes, Guacali, Macocoma, Mamuya, Manos Sordos, Mapoch, Mesquite, Pajarito, Piedras Blancas, Pinole, Polacme Satatu, Siniple, Sinoreja, Suahuache, Suana, Tapachuache, Obozi, Piedras Blancas, Hiabu, Cenizo, Ismiquilpa, Mahuame, Xarame, Chaquantie, Pachaloco, Pakawa, Tet, Ervipiame, Mariame, Muruam, Rancheria Grande, Pasqual, Pitalac, Pomulum, Teaname, Xeripam, Ybacax, Yemé, Ymic, Ysbupue, Tamcan, Sijame, Siupam, Tusolivi, Yojuane, Mescal, Nacachau, Nacau, Nacogdoche, Nacono, Neche, Pamaya, Saracuam, Nasoni, Nacachau, Ervipiame, Huyuguan, Manos Prietas, Payaya, Piniquu, Terocodame, Xarame, Caux, Nasoni, Sama, Sumi, Tonkawa, Wichita, Kichai, Nacaniche, Yscani, Natchitoch, Aguastaya, Camama, Cana, Pastia, Payuguan, Sulujame, Apache, Deadose, Aranama, Coapite, Cujane, Taracone, Muruam, Nonapho, Pampopa, Pasalve, Patacal, Pita, Quanataguo, Tucara, Tumpzi, Tacame, Nigco, Pajalat, Sepuncó, Taztasagonie, Orejone, Pajalat, Siquipil, Tilijae, Tilpacopal, Tiopane, Venado, Chenti, Lipan, Ervipiame, Yxandi, Patalca, Pachalaque, Patumaca, Parchina, Pelone, Arahoma, Sencase, Tacame, Tinapihuaya, Pausane, Cava Menenquen, Tenu, Tetzino, Toho, Ujuiap, Zorquan, Paguanan, Pasnacanes, Pajaseque, Anathagua, Anchose, Apapax, Atia, Atiasnogue, Cancepne, Caso, Geote, Mayeye, Pastate, Yojuane, Akokisa, Bidai, Patiri, Tamique, Emet, Esquien, Estepisa, Tup, Tiopine, Chayopine.

—Source: *Chronology of Texas History,* Donald W. Whisenhunt, Eakin Press, 1982

Spain Founds El Paso

In 1598 Spain decided to look for riches and for Native Americans who could be converted to Christianity in today's New Mexico. **Don Juan Oñate,** a wealthy silver mine heir whose wife was a descendant of both Cortés and Montezuma, won the position of governor and captain general of the new territory. Oñate gathered up quite an entourage—hundreds of settlers, tradesmen, and civil servants, including 130 families. They piled up 83 wagons and carts, collected 7,000 cattle, and headed out of Santa Barbara, in the south part of today's Mexican state of Chihuahua, and marched across the Chihuahua desert to the present location of San Elizario, Texas, where Oñate claimed for King Phillip II all the territory drained by the Rio Grande. **He passed through what is now downtown El Paso** and went on to found Spanish settlements in New Mexico. These settlements are also important in the settlement of Texas, for when the Indians rebelled eighty-four years later, some of the refugees who fled south started the settlement of **Ysleta.**

Escandón

One hundred and fifty years later, and three-quarters of a century before Stephen F. Austin's Old Three Hundred colonized Texas from the east, a highly respected Spaniard, **José de Escandón,** mounted a major colonizing expedition from the south. Escandón was born in 1700 in Soto Merissa, Spain, and his title was El Conde de la Sierra Gorda. On December 2, 1748, he left Querétaro, Mexico, with **750 soldiers and 2,500 settlers** and Christianized Indians. This huge force, whose dust cloud could have been seen from the moon, moved steadily across 400 miles of the Sierra Madre and desert until it reached the Rio Grande. On the south side of the Rio Grande, Escandón founded Camargo (1749), Reynosa (1749), Mier (1753), and Revilla (Guerrero, 1753). On the north side of the river he founded **Laredo,** now in Texas. All these towns still exist. More settlers moved in from south and west of the Lower Rio

Grande—the stretch between present-day Laredo and Brownsville—to settle on both sides of the river. Later, when political factions divided their interests at the river, those on the south found themselves in the Mexican state of Tamaulipas, while those on the north were in Texas. This division did not sever the deep cultural and familial bonds between the two. They kept their traditions.

San Antonio

The Spaniards divided their settlements into three parts: military (presidio), town (pueblo), and religious (mission). San Antonio is an example. The mission, **San Antonio de Valero** (later known as the Alamo), was established in 1718. At the same time, the military established its **Presidio San Antonio de Béjar** nearby. In 1730 colonists from the **Canary Islands** settled the area around the town of **Pueblo de San Fernando.** Collectively, these entities became our vibrant **San Antonio,** second largest city in Texas, with a population of more than one million. In 1968 San Antonio celebrated its 250th birthday by hosting *HemisFair*, an exposition attended by more than six million people from around the world.

Vaqueros were part of a larger cattle-herding culture that in two centuries had spread throughout Spanish America. They inherited their saddles and other gear, horsemanship, and methods for handling herds from Spain. They took different names as they spread through the New World, but they stayed essentially the same: **they rode horses to cover a lot of territory, and they herded cattle** descended from those brought by the Conquistadors, often driving them great distances to feed or water them, or deliver them to market. Here are some of the names the vaqueros were known by:

> *chalán*—Peru
>> cowboy—U.S. and Canada
>>> *criollos*—Spaniards born in the Americas
>>>> *gaucho*—Argentina and Uruguay
>>>>> *gaúcho*—Brazil
>>>>>> *huaso*—Chile
>>>>>>> *llanero*—Colombia and Venezuela
>>>>>>>> *vaquero*—Mexico

Their essential tools were Spanish spurs, bits, stirrups, and saddles. They all had smaller tools made from leather, horn, or wood, such as the *rebenque,* a flat lash; *boleadoras,* a device for entangling the legs of animals, of Brazil and Andean South America; and the *quirt*, a short, usually round-plaited whip used in Texas and the rest of the U.S. The *chifle* is a canteen used in Argentina, made from cow horn. In all these countries, the vaqueros and their brethren became folk heroes representing daring, virility, and patriotism. Their way of life inspired adventurous, robust literature, similar in many ways to stories of the Knights Errant brought over by the first Spaniards. On January 16, 1748, **Texas's first cattle brand** was issued to Joseph de Estrados. In the **first big roundup,** or *corrida,* thirty-nine years later, *vaqueros* from many widely spread ranches, mostly in today's South Texas, gathered cattle and drove the herds east to Lousiana and south across the Rio Grande to be sold and traded.

The Anglo-American Tide

Hard economic times often become an impetus for people to move on. The economic realities of the early 1800s in the U.S. set the stage for another wave of migration to Texas. General economic difficulties worsened with the Panic of

1819 and the tight money policies of the federal government. Large numbers of people suffered humiliating foreclosures and lawsuits, and even imprisonment, for debts. Because there were no bankruptcy laws to protect them from creditors, many people suffered total ruin.

Moses Austin and his son, **Stephen Fuller Austin,** suffered through these hard economic times in Virginia, Missouri, and Arkansas. But in the midst of these hardships, **Moses, an energetic visionary and entrepreneur, prepared Stephen to be a leading citizen of the world.** By example, he taught his son not to give up in the face of adversity and to be forward looking. Moses, as Stephen learned, always had a new and bigger project in mind whenever one project failed—and this would have implications for the future of Texas.

The Austins had tried to develop Little Rock, Arkansas, in 1820, but it was a difficult time to be in business. Stephen, who had been appointed judge of Arkansas's First Circuit Court, was amazed at the unethical conduct among land speculators. They were driven nearly rabid by the chance for quick profits. As Stephen put it, "I have learnt to be surprised at nothing I see in man, unless it is when I find him honest."

Meanwhile, there was also instability further west and south in Mexico (which included present-day Texas). Americans had been aware of the independence movement in Mexico since 1810. The Magee Expedition took control of Texas in 1812 and 1813, but was defeated. Then in 1819, the James Long Expedition again invaded and controlled some parts of Texas. Spain, which ruled Mexico, was unstable itself. For two centuries it had been unable to establish enough of a population in Coahuila y Texas and New Mexico to ensure that the vast area would be loyal to the crown.

This political instability in Mexico and the economic challenges in the United States—including the severe recession that hit New Orleans, the great port of the Gulf of Mexico, in 1821—triggered another of Moses Austin's brainstorms. (Moses was now living in Missouri and Stephen in New Orleans.)

Exasperated with the seizure of his property by creditors and the lack of new business opportunities, he like many other business people, sought refuge and a new start in Texas.

Moses Austin's Last Big Deal

Accompanied by Richmond, the family slave, Moses took his rifle and pistol, and **set out across the uncharted territory west of Louisiana.** He had already dealt with the Spanish crown when he secured the right to mine lead on a large tract near today's St. Louis. Now he planned to meet the provincial governor at San Antonio de Béjar and make an offer that, hopefully, the governor could not refuse. Moses gained an audience with the governor and proposed that he be allowed to bring Anglo colonists into Texas. The governor, Antonio Martínez, ordered Austin to get out of Texas and stay out.

On his way out of the plaza, however, Moses ran into Baron de Bastrop, a businessman he had met many years earlier in New Orleans. The baron, after several unsuccessful ventures, had wound up as a well-respected citizen of San Antonio. A couple of days later, the two reappeared before the governor with a proposal to colonize a section of Texas with three hundred Catholic families from the United States. Now Martínez listened. In his short time as governor, he had been unable to bring any significant number of Mexican families to the province; they weren't interested in relocating to such an isolated place. Martínez recommended the plan to his superiors in Monterrey, Mexico.

Moses and Richmond headed for home. They barely made it to Natchitoches, Louisiana, alive. A traveling companion stole their horses, gear, and food. The two lived off the land and survived an attack by a cougar. They eventually made it back home to Missouri. Although exhausted, Moses worked hard to get his affairs in order so he could return to Texas. However, he came down with a fever, and after a few days with his wife and several doctors at his bedside, he died on June 10, 1821.

His plan to colonize Texas was carried out after his death by his son, Stephen. Though Stephen did not lead a caravan of settlers to Texas, he did advertise in newspapers and wrote letters, saying that settlers would receive land, liberal privileges in commerce, and civil rights. He must have been convincing, because the colonists simply showed up in San Felipe de Austin (very near where the Brazos River crosses today's Interstate 10) where Stephen had built himself a cabin.

Music for Mother

Many settlers travelled vast distances to the new land. This migration invariably left loved ones "back there." Returning home to Appalachia or the East Coast was too difficult for most to achieve. Such pestilences as yellow fever and malaria struck suddenly. One never knew whether a good-bye was the final one. **Yearning for home was a common theme expressed in music.** In 1910, the Trio Music Company of Waco published several such songs in a little book called *Carols of Victory*. Here's a verse called *The Songs That Mother Sang*:

> The dear old songs I love so well,
> Are those that mother sang:
> When her sweet voice in melody
> Throughout the old home rang.
> The dear old songs, the dear old songs, that mother sang.
>
> —*R.E. Campbell*

And this verse, from *Mother and Home:*

> Years ago when but a boy,
> Singing songs was mother's joy,
> When my father dear would leave us there so lone;
> I can hear her voice so sweet,
> As she'd sing "When shall we meet,"

I can ne'er forget my mother and my home.

My dear mother, she was true

To her children and her home;

she was patient, tender, kind, and lov'd us all;

I praise God for her sweet name.

She was ever just the same;

I can ne'er forget my mother and my home.

—W.J. Laney

History in a Nutshell

Mexico won its independence from Spain in 1821. **Texans won their independence from Mexico in 1836.** Texas remained an independent republic until 1845, when it joined the United States. Texas withdrew from the Union in 1861 to join the Confederate States of America. After the South lost the Civil War (1861–65), Texas was returned to the Union, where it has been ever since.

Emancipation

Juneteenth, celebrated on June 19 every year, is a uniquely Texas celebration of a great event. **On June 19, 1865, 250,000 enslaved African Americans in Texas received the news that they were free.** That's when Union General Gordon Granger read the Emancipation Proclamation in Galveston. Some of the early emancipation festivities were relegated by white city authorities to each town's outskirts. In time, however, groups of African Americans collected money until they had enough to buy land for their celebrations, including Juneteenth. A common name for these sites was Emancipation Park.

Helping Hands

Joshua Houston (1822–1902) was born in slavery in Alabama on the plantation of Temple Lea. Lea's daughter, Margaret, who inherited Joshua, married Sam Houston and took Joshua and the rest of his family to Texas in 1934 when Joshua was twelve. Joshua traveled with Sam and was a servant in the Governor's Mansion, where he met most of the important people of the time. Sam and Margaret saw that he learned to read and write, and encouraged him to work at an independent job driving a stagecoach, which he did. He saved much of the money he earned.

After Sam died in 1863, Margaret was broke (Sam left her land, but he had no money to bequeath), so Joshua offered her his $2,000 savings in gold. She refused it, urging him to spend it on educating his children. He did, and several of them had distinguished careers. **Joshua Houston became a civic leader in Huntsville,** where he built a house and a blacksmith shop, and served as deacon of his church (Baptist, like Sam and Margaret). He served as alderman, county commissioner, and a delegate to the 1888 Republican Convention.

80 John

D. W. "80 John" Wallace was a legendary African-American cattleman from Mitchell County. A former slave, he worked for Clay Mann, and took on Mann's "80" brand as a nickname. With Mann's encouragement, 80 John built up his own cattle herds and started buying ranch land. After Clay Mann died, he took over management of Mann's ranch for Mann's wife. By the end of his life, **80 John had accumulated 8,000 acres in two counties,** and each of his four children had completed college. Public buildings in Colorado City are named for him, and he has his own historical marker.

Texas Czechs

Czech influence is strongly felt in Texas, especially in a cluster of fifteen counties between Dallas and Austin. The Czech presence is also strong in those counties southeast of Austin that served as the receiving colonies for the migrations of Moravian and Bohemian families. These migrations started in 1851, following the failure of the European revolutions of 1848.

One Reverend Josef Arnost Bergmann came from Europe to serve a German Protestant congregation in Cat Spring in Austin County, fittingly located only a few miles from San Felipe de Austin, the government seat of Stephen F. Austin's first colony. The good minister wrote a letter home praising this new country for its ethnic freedom and availability of good farmland. The letter was published in a newspaper in Moravia and was widely read by a people, suppressed for their ethnic identity, who were living in an overcrowded land.

After voyages that lasted more than three months, groups of Czechs—mostly Catholic—arrived in the years 1851–54, dispersing from Cat Spring to surrounding areas, including **Fayetteville, which became the Czech's main economic and cultural center.** The first all-Czech communities in Texas are said to have been Dubina or Hostyn; other towns, such as New Ulm, Schulenburg, Ellinger, La Grange, Nelsonville, and Wesley still retain the flavor of this culture.

The Czechs have not allowed their culture to be assimilated into the city cultures as much as other ethnic groups. They have maintained their characteristic painted churches, music, and festivals in those original communities so well that, collectively, they have become known as "Czech country." In addition, the Czechs have influenced the cuisine of Texas in one highly noticeable and delightful way: their *kolaches*, pastries usually containing fruit fillings, are enjoyed all over Texas.

Czech population climbed to about 700 by the Civil War. Other groups of Czechs immigrated in the 1870s and 1880s and shortly after 1900. The number of Texans listing some Czech ancestry in the 1990 census was nearly 300,000, but some Czech organizations put the number closer to a million.

Czechs contributed the music of their polkas and waltzes—and especially the sound of their accordion—to the Hispanic culture, which assimilated them into its Tejano music.

Where We Live

Physical

Elevations range from sea level to more than 8,000 feet. Rainfall ranges from 8 inches of moisture per year in the desert regions of West Texas to more than 55 inches annually in East Texas.

Just Look at the Shape We're In

*"Texas is situated on the map of the United States **as a keel is on a racing yacht**. It keeps the country goin' straight."*

—Source: Anonymous

Surveyors took the measure of Texas with chains, using a Spanish unit of measurement called a *vara*. A *vara* is 33.33 inches long. **A fifty-vara survey chain was so heavy it took two men to carry it.** Surveyors could lay out ten or twelve miles a day depending on the terrain. That was how the political boundaries of Texas were laid out, fifty varas at a time. A marker was set at the corner of each one-square-mile section (640 acres). These markers then served settlers as guide and compass. Settlers crossing the featureless plains also guided on buffalo wallows, each of which had a unique shape. Common people of

earlier centuries were more familiar with the night sky than most of us are today for the simple reason that they spent more time outside. Most could guide on the constellations at night, and were familiar with how they moved around during the year.

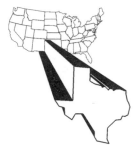

If you had a long enough string or a big enough pair of compasses to draw a circle 801 miles in diameter, Texas would fit in it. In fact, 28 miles would be left over in the east-to-west direction, because the state is slightly taller than it is wide. We have four major physical regions: the Gulf Coast Plains, the Interior Lowlands, the Great Plains, and the Basin and Range Province. That's what the books say. My guess is, not twenty Texans out of twenty million (unless they wrote one of the books) could tell you precisely where these areas start and leave off. Not that Texans are unaware. It's that we have different ways of referring to these places, and the farther away we are from them, the more generalized our references get. Furthermore, these four major regions are divided into a lot of smaller regions.

Take the Gulf Coastal Plains. Within it you will find such areas as the Lower Rio Grande Valley (which is a plain and not a valley), the Rio Grande Plain, the Coastal Prairies, the Post Oak Belt, the Pine Belt, and not one, but two Blackland Belts. Other regions have their own particulates: within Texas's portion of the Great Plains, I find not only the Staked Plains, but the Toyah Basin, the Stockton Plateau, the Edwards Plateau, and the Llano Basin. I've had friends

and family members who lived in all those places, and without exception, they would have thought I was some kind of uneducated city slicker if I had used any of those names in casual conversation.

In the nearly unknown (as far as the rest of the world is concerned) Interior Lowlands, there are the North Central Plains, the Western Cross Timbers, the Grand Prairie, and the eastern Cross Timbers. Rather than keep up with all these elevated cognomens, we have kept to our forebears' ways of giving out directions. We're likely to say something like, "Oh that would be out around El Paso," or "Up around Amarillo," or "Down at Houston." If we farm, we're likely to tell you which county's loam our tractor plows.

With the **Compromise of 1850**, the United States "bought" sections of New Mexico, Colorado, Oklahoma, and Kansas from Texas for $10 million.

Texas administered **Greer County** until 1896, when the United States Supreme Court ruled an old survey invalid. The surveyor had picked the wrong tributary of the Red River. Greer County then switched from being a Texas county to being a territory of the United States. In 1906 it became part of the new state of Oklahoma. So the Texas Panhandle used to be a lot fatter on the east.

Ysleta, established in 1682 by refugees fleeing south to escape the Indian revolt in New Mexico, was not always in Texas. Ysleta was in Mexico until the **Rio Grande changed its course** from the east side to the west side of town. Ysleta wound up in El Paso County.

The **Nueces Strip**, that long, narrow piece of ground in South Texas that lies between the Rio Grande and the Nueces River, was called **Wild Horse Desert**. "Immense Herds of Wild Horses," the maps of 1836 said. The mustangs, descendants of those lost three hundred years earlier by expeditions such as that of Coronado in 1540–42, were as numerous as buffalo and passenger pigeons. Texas and Mexico argued over who owned the Strip. That issue and many others were settled with the capture of Santa Anna and the destruction of his army at San Jacinto in 1836.

Mirabeau Bounaparte Lamar, the second president of the Republic of Texas, the "Father of Texas Education," thought Texas extended to the Pacific Ocean, and was never asked to teach geography.

The point in Texas **farthest west** is located on **Chuck Loper's dairy farm** 1.25 miles south and 2.6 miles west of Canutillo. There's a bronze survey marker (placed in 1928) in a yard next to the house where Shirley and Virgil Phillips, Chuck's aunt and uncle, live. The bedrooms are in Texas, and the kitchen is in New Mexico.

Subdividing

At the time of **Mexico's independence from Spain in 1821,** there were three municipalities in Texas: San Fernando de Béxar, today's San Antonio; La Bahía del Espirito Santo, today's Goliad; and in Nacogdoches, East Texas.

Coahuila, still a Mexican state, was joined to Texas in 1824, and the resulting political state was called *Coahuila y Texas*. Within this state Texas became the Department of Béxar, administered in San Antonio. This department was divided into twenty-three municipalities, each of which could include one or more towns and associated territory.

★ ★

Georgia O'Keeffe, that mystical, terrific painter of cow skulls and calla lilies, came to Canyon to teach at West Texas State Normal College (now West Texas A&M University) in 1916. O'Keeffe was well acquainted with the big city—she had spent plenty of time in New York and Chicago—but with her first look at the great open sky and plains of the Texas Panhandle, she loved the place. Here are some of the elements she described in her letters:

the prairie, like an ocean

the Palo Duro Canyon so deep cows looked like
pinheads in the bottom of it

windmills

grey-blue clouds

jack rabbits in headlights

and the SKY, such a SKY

The governing body for each municipality (which, since it often included more than one town, was similar to our county) was the *ayuntamiento*, usually made up of a representative from each of five segments of officialdom. The five members were:

the *alcalde* from the judicial branch

the *alguacil*, or sheriff

the *escribano*, the scribe or secretary for the *ayuntamiento*

the *regidores*, representatives of town councils (*cabildos*)

the *sindico procurador*, prosecuting attorney

After Texas became a republic in 1836, the twenty-three municipal districts became counties in the pattern followed in the southern United States. For several years the justices of the peace and the chief justice governed the county; in 1845 four commissioners replaced the JPs. Later still, the chief justice became the county judge.

Community Road Building

The main duty for the county administrators was to build new roads and maintain the existing ones. During this time, all free males ages 18–45 and slaves ages 16–50 had to work on the roads.

This arrangement, in general, lasted into the twentieth century. In Scurry County, through the 1920s a boy could apply for permission to work in place of his father; similarly, a man could receive labor credit for using his own wagon to help in the roadwork.

A typical assignment started with a letter from the county commissioners setting out the time and location at which to appear. When the workers assembled, a foreman took stock of the number of workers, wagons, draft horses, scrapers, and so on, and gave out assignments, usually starting with sending the wagons to a proscribed location for caliche, sand, or gravel with which to patch holes in the dirt roads.

This community service gave participants a sense of ownership in their countryside that few recognized until many years later. One day in the early 1990s, I was on a landmark-visiting trip with **Herman Elkins** of Kent and Scurry counties, who related with obvious pride how, some sixty-odd years before, **he had helped create the road we were driving on.** "Scraped the brush off, cut the bar ditches, hauled and shoveled the caliche, then came back the next year and filled up the holes. People sure got from one side of the county to the other a lot quicker after we built that road." Herman looked out serenely at his handiwork and puffed on his pipe, a job well done.

Counties, Counties, Everywhere

The republic, eager to set up governing structures to keep pace with settlement, created **fifty new counties during the 1830s,** starting a process that took nearly ninety years to complete. The state organized **sixty-six counties during the 1850s,** and by the end of that decade organized counties fronted all along the 100th parallel. More settlers joined the rage to move to Texas, and when they got here they looked approvingly across that invisible line at the country still to come. If you draw a line straight down the east side of the Panhandle (which is the 100th parallel) and continue it until it intersects the Rio Grande about fifty miles upstream from Laredo, you will have an idea of what the political map of Texas looked like at the time. (Remember, though, that from 1821 until the 1850 Compromise, Texas considered all of today's New Mexico and parts of Colorado, Kansas, and Oklahoma to be within its boundaries.)

During the 1860s only six additional counties were organized, a process slowed by the Civil War and Indian depredations while troops were out of the state. After the Comanches were forced to move to reservations in the 1870s, county building resumed. **The process continued until 1931 when Loving became the 254th Texas county.** Bexar ended her long role as the mother county of Texas with 128 offspring.

A favorite place: Jordan's Plant Farm southwest of Henderson. Eighty-two greenhouses, an old-time hotel, general store, post office, kitchen, barber shop, church, school, hotel lobby, and saloon. Jordan's produces more than 40,000 poinsettias for Christmas.

In a larger sense, **our feelings for community** extend well past our state lines. Many of us regularly visit our families and friends in Mexico, New Mexico, Oklahoma, Arkansas, and Louisiana. We easily drive from East Texas to Shreveport to "shoe our horses" on the riverboats. And we welcome the winter Texans who enrich our southern clime with both their money and their many acts of kindness. Not long ago I visited a preschool classroom in Mission, where a physics professor and his wife from Minnesota served as volunteers every day. It was obvious the children, whom they were helping learn to read, considered them basic necessities.

How Lavaca County Got to Be Itself

In 1831, thirty-three land grants were awarded by Stephen F. Austin and Green C. DeWitt for families who would establish homes in the area.

In 1833 **John Hallet built a log cabin** alongside the Lavaca River, then went back home to Goliad, where he died in 1836. Hallet's wife, Margaret, set up a store in his log cabin. People started calling the place, guess what? Halletsville! For six years the population grew.

In 1842 the Texas Congress (while Texas was independent), created a county from pieces of five counties, and named the new county LaBaca, which shortly became Lavaca. Two towns, Petersburg and Hallettsville, wanted to be the county seat. After two elections and some fisticuffs, Halletsville won. After the Civil War, Czechs and Germans began settling the county, creating the agricultural and cultural richness it enjoys today.

If you were a resident of a new area that wasn't a county yet, **it was in your best interest to try to create a county,** so you wouldn't have to send your tax money far away. Nor would you have to spend days or weeks tramping across hills and hollows trying to avoid Comanches, rattlesnakes, northers, and tornadoes to file your legal papers or get your marriage license. After Texas became a state, the legislature made up some general rules stating that in order to be considered, your proposed county had to have at least 150 citizens, and the county seat must be no more than one day's round-trip from the farthest part. This round-trip rule calculated out to a square 30 miles on a side, or 900 square miles. That's why you see all those orderly squares up in the Panhandle and south nearly to Central Texas.

This method of **drawing a new county on a piece of paper** did have its unforeseen consequences. In Armstrong County, Wayside is on one side of the Palo Duro Canyon and Claude, the county seat, is on the other.

And of course, by now you've got really smart looking at the map of the state of Texas and you've noticed that out west in the Trans-Pecos, those counties sure aren't thirty-mile squares. Take for instance, **Brewster, the largest county in Texas.** It's nowhere near a square and it covers about 6,000 square miles, forty-two times the area of our smallest county, Rockwall, and five times the area of Rhode Island. Why so big? I bet I know the explanation: they raised faster horses out there and the landscape's flatter. They got started early, rode

hard, and put 'em up late. I'm sure that's the answer. Um, probably not. If you figure this out, tell someone who knows me and they can tell me.

Instant Towns

Colorado City began shortly before the Texas & Pacific Railroad reached the site. The owners of Dunn, Coleman, and Company rushed out ahead of the railroad construction and, guessing where it would pass, built a store at a site where early suppliers had sold merchandise to buffalo hunters. This was in August of 1880. They guessed right. The first train arrived eight months later, and with the establishment of quarters for the construction crew, more than five hundred other entrepreneurs arrived with their tents folded up on the back of their wagons and set about creating—civilization! The next month, May 1881, city lots were surveyed and sold. Lumber came in on the train, and the citizens began to replace their tents with frame buildings. The Texas & Pacific built loading pens outside of town for cattle, and **Colorado City quickly became the greatest shipping center for the cattle business in Texas.** Cowmen drove their herds in from a radius of two hundred miles—a far easier trek than they had been used to, which had taken them all the way to Kansas through Indian country. That same year citizens enjoyed a horse-drawn street car, a race track, and a zoo. Known variously as the Dodge City of the Southwest, the Queen of the West, and the Mother City of West Texas, Colorado City in 1884 had twenty-eight saloons, seventy-five merchants, two photographers, seven pool halls, four theaters, three real estate agents, twelve lawyers, one barber, seven peddlers, two lightning rod agents, and one dentist.

First Telegraph

The first telegraph office in Texas was opened in Marshall on Valentine's Day 1854, by the Texas & Red River Telegraph Company. It was connected to

lines from New Orleans and Shreveport, Louisiana, and Natchez, Mississippi. By 1862 1,000 miles of telegraph line was operating in Texas. The military installed a southern transcontinental line, which was completed in Texas in 1877. The lines through East Texas were attached to pine trees. After high winds, if the telegraph wouldn't work, the operators had to close their offices to ride out and fix the lines broken by swaying trees.

First Hello

Colonel A.H. Belo, publisher of the *Galveston News,* noticed Alexander Graham Bell's invention at the Philadelphia Centennial Exposition in 1876. On March 18, 1878, a line was installed between his newspaper office and his home, and **the first telephone in Texas,** and one of the first 1,000 anywhere, was installed. Of course, to make it work, there were probably two. Or maybe the Colonel didn't understand how the thing worked? Hello? Hello?

In 1922, the Belo company started broadcasting from the first network-affiliated radio station in the state. In 1998, Belo's WFAA television station was the first VHF station to transmit a digital signal as a permanent vehicle for its programming, and in 1999 it inaugurated Texas Cable NEW (TXCN), the first around-the-clock cable news channel serving a region in Texas. The same company published the first newspaper, the *Galveston News,* in 1842. Today it publishes the *Dallas Morning News.* The Belo company has operated continuously longer than any other company in the state.

Modern Conveniences

Our folks had a flock of geese. We caught them two times a year and picked their feathers and down. We made feather pillows and down comforts. We put the head of the goose in a tow sack and held it tight around his neck so he couldn't bite the one doing the picking.

In about 1936 or '37, we moved from a two-room boxcar shack into a new house. Our new home had three bedrooms, a living room, a dining room, kitchen and breakfast nook, an enclosed back porch, a long hall, a basement, and a bathroom. In a few years our daddy installed a kerosene hot-water heater. We were so very proud of this. Daddy would ask at noon who wanted a bath that night. If at least three of us wanted a bath, he would light the kerosene hot-water heater. That was a real luxury having hot running water for a bath.

In about 1939 we got a 32-volt wind charger. This was absolutely great. This system had thirty-two batteries set up on a shelf in the basement. The first battery had three different colored balls in it. If the three balls were at the top, we could iron with the electric iron. If not, we had to iron with the old flat irons heated on the stove. This system also allowed us to have a radio. Daddy would time his milking the cows to allow him to listen to *Amos and Andy*. Progress was coming quickly. We had a new Servel refrigerator and could make ice. We got butane and could have a gas cook stove and gas hot-water heater in the kitchen. We also got a rug for the living room floor. Now we were really living in style.

At first our home was white stucco. To take advantage of our grandfather's talent of being a rock mason, it was decided to rock our house and our daddy's brother's house. Our daddy hauled the rock for both houses from the country around Snyder, Texas.

At this time a black man by the name of Jessie Lee worked with our daddy. While Daddy was hauling rock, I became very ill with high fever. Jessie Lee was concerned and thought I had the measles and could not break out. So he gathered dried corn shucks from the barn and boiled them, and I was given hot corn shuck tea to drink. Within six hours I was broken out solid with measles.

We got a new 1941 Pontiac car—this car had to last through World War II. Gas was rationed so we saved our ration stamps to buy gas to go to my grandmother's and uncle's twenty-seven miles south of Big Lake. They got raw sugar and coffee from Old Mexico. The sugar was dark and coarse but sweet. Almost everything that we had to buy was scarce. We had ration stamps for lots of items— coffee, sugar, shoes, gas, tires, but we did not mind because we would have given up almost anything to help in the war effort. We and almost every one of our neighbors and friends and people in business were very patriotic.

We grew large gardens and canned almost all of what we ate. In addition to vegetables, we canned cooked sausage in fruit jars because the sausage would get old before we could use it. Because I had small hands that would go into a canning jar, my job was to wash jars—hundreds of them. One of the best things we canned was pickled peaches. Many a day when I got off the school bus, I went to the basement and got a cold jar of pickled peaches—my mom made the best! My oldest brother and I would eat a quart jar full of pickled peaches at one setting.

Almost all farmers had large flocks of chickens. In the summer the chickens roosted in trees around the chicken house and barnyard. In the fall they had to be driven into the chicken house to prepare for a cold winter. A neighbor wanted my brother and me to help drive his chickens into his chicken house—there is nothing as crazy as a bunch of chickens. They would just as soon fly right into your face as not. We worked at the dirty job for about two hours. The neighbors were so very thankful that the dirty job was done that she treated us. She divided a six-ounce Coke between us.

—DORIS DURRETT, *ABERNATHY*

Railroads and Moveable Towns

In 1899 the Pecos and Northern Texas Railway built through the southern part of Deaf Smith County and into New Mexico, but not through the town of La Plata, the county seat. Well! This development was highly disappointing to those who had built houses and stores and set up farms, counting on La Plata being the center of things. Some of its citizens strolled over to **the new town of Bluewater, that *was* on the railroad,** and looked around enviously. Here were these new rails shining silver in the sun, and here were these store owners about to make some money, and here were these railroad cars rattling up that you could just load your cattle or your crops on and send them off to market. Right here was where the action was going to be. These solid citizens strolled back home, probably chewing on straws. "Well, Luke, what do you think of that? Does it look to you like we're mostly just flat out of luck?" And Luke thought that, Yes, there just wasn't any other way to look at it. This railroad was going to open up the country. Why, you could get on that thing and be in Dallas in no time at all.

The idea of A New Global Economic Order occurred to these farmers and shopkeepers that day on their stroll back to La Plata. As they approached their town, it looked so pitiful, so isolated and lonesome, its cluster of plank buildings gathered up as if for protection from the cold. On November 8 of that year, the citizens of La Plata chose a new county seat, and it was that other town, Bluewater. Shortly after the election, all the able-bodied farmers and merchants got up early to load up their wagons with hammers and saws and pry bars. Then they hitched their mules to their wagons and drove into the middle of Main Street. By this time it was coming daylight. They had already talked over what

they were going to do, and in the manner of country people of that day, they didn't talk much. **By nightfall they had moved all nine houses, the courthouse, and the jail over to Bluewater.**

At first, railroads used track put together in joints—not welded. But **jointed tracks produced a rough ride** up in the passenger cars, so now the tracks are welded. **Welded tracks allow a smooth ride,** but don't allow room for expansion when the weather gets hot. The result is misalignment, or "sun kinks." When the temperature reaches 80 degrees F., railroad inspectors check the tracks every three or four days. At 100 degrees, the inspectors are out there every day.

Crashed by Crush

G.W. Crush, a passenger agent for the Missouri, Kansas, and Texas Railroad, had an idea.** He thought, "Here we are, we've got all this railroad track, and we've got all these locomotives, and we've got all these empty passenger cars. We need something to get paying passengers interested in riding the train." Crush had a great imagination, and he was always coming up with ideas to improve the MK&T. He decided the people needed a real spectacle, something no one had ever done, and something that little kids with toys were always doing. How about, Crush thought, **stoking up two steam locomotives** as hot as their boilers would go, and turning them loose at one another. What if, he thought, you gave them a good long run so they were going as fast as a locomotive could possibly go, and had them collide right in front of a string of passenger cars all filled with customers? Could he sell tickets? Does a frog jump? G.W. Crush got cranking. The upper echelon thought it was a whingdinger of an idea, one that would make MK&T better known than the Union Pacific. G.W. picked out a spot between Waco and the small community of West, started hawking tickets, and by crash day had 50,000 paying passengers that he brought in on 30 passenger cars. On September 15, 1896, when the two locomotives collided, the boilers exploded, killing two people and injuring several more. The MK&T paid off the survivors, and no one ever tried *that* trick again.

Further On

And they moved. They heard of a better place farther along. Cattlemen would live in a place a few years until the "boys" needed land of their own. **Most families were not from somewhere for very long.** That's the way it was in an expanding economy, in a system finding its equilibrium. It seemed no one was satisfied. They followed opportunity. They wanted better homes and care for their families. The rural Southerners who had been sharecroppers moved into new cotton country, helping build gins and run hotels and other businesses. In the East Texas pine forests, the farmers moved into the new mill towns, and then moved from one mill town to the other. One sawmill manager said he ran three crews. One working, one leaving, and one arriving.

When folks moved, they often left many family members behind them in the ground. Smallpox took away whole families during the 1880s. A family named Fiveash was taken in the space of a few days. Their small cemetery, surrounded by a simple iron fence, stands alongside a rural road in Coleman County. We wonder who was left to bury them. In nearby Mitchell County lies the Iatan cemetery, the loneliest burying ground in all that wide country. Shards of glass and pottery, all that's left of bud vases and ceramic lambs, mark the sand where babies are buried who died in the 1918 influenza epidemic. Too many little markers say it all: *Gone too soon.*

Major George Washington Littlefield, a solid, philanthropic businessman who, during the Civil War, had fought at Shiloh, Chicamauga, and Lookout Mountain with Terry's Texas Rangers, bought 225,858 acres, built a model town, and invited prospective farmers to come, admire, and purchase—on good terms—a piece of the flattest, most fertile ground any of them had ever seen. Those who came in late summer could see the proof. Littlefield put in a model farm—complete with a windmill pumping streams of crystal water from the Ogallala Aquifer—which produced huge melons, magnificent golden corn, and heaping bushels of beans, peas, okra, squash, and tomatoes.

Church Services in a New Town

In Clarendon in 1885, **the Reverend W. A. Cooper** conducted a church service for a few Methodists, an Episcopalian family, a few cowboys, and Morris "Rosie" Rosenfield, a Jew, who provided a beautiful vocal solo. Rosie was a partner in the general store. The large iron bell that signaled the time for church had been brought from Chicago by the previous minister. The bell was hung on a scaffold so that a person standing on the ground could ring it. It was the job of a boy whose family lived up a draw several miles away to get to town early enough to ring the bell.

In 1858, the Methodist church at Plehweville—now the Art Community in Mason County—**set the salary of its pastor at nine dollars every three months.** This was a a mighty fine deal, seeing as how his congregation kept him supplied with meat, eggs, vegetables, and fruit.

Nancy Moffette Lea, mother-in-law of President Sam Houston, was one of the organizers of the Baptist Church in Texas.

Ernest Durrett's Tour of Duty

I was living at home on my family's farm near Abernathy, Texas, when I was drafted into the army in April 1945. I was twenty years old. I rode a bus about 350 miles to the induction center in El Paso, and from there to Camp Maxie at Paris, Texas, for seventeen weeks of basic training. The war in the Pacific had ended by this time because of the dropping of the atomic bomb. The army sent me home on furlow, then I reported to Camp Stowman at Monterey, California. At Camp Stowman we were issued rifles and infantry equipment, then sent to San Francisco where we boarded a troop ship. We were on board the ship thirteen days and nights, and part of this time we were in a typhoon.

When we arrived in Yokohama, Japan, in September 1945, we were sent to the Fourth Replacement Depot for assignment. As the fighting there was over, I was sent to the 37th General Hospital near downtown Tokyo, where I was assigned to work on the contagious disease ward. Since we were the first occupation troops in Japan, we had been trained for the infantry. We had no medical training, so I learned by doing.

This was not a bad experience. If you worked for the good of your patients and followed guidelines, you were given more authority and responsibility. Two of my neighbors from home who had joined the navy, Lyndel Myatt and Donald Blackmon, came to the hospital to visit and have Thanksgiving and Christmas dinner with me. They enjoyed the reunion, but mainly they came because the hospital served better food than they got with the navy. Back home, Lyndel lived on a farm about two miles northwest of our place, and Donald lived farther over toward Shallowater.

I often went to downtown Tokyo, where there were small Japanese shops. I bought silk yard goods and tablecloths, lace, oriental kimonos, and cameras to send home. We were also near General Douglas MacArthur's Supreme Allied Headquarters. If you wanted to stand and wait for him, you could watch him come out of the building and get in his chauffered car and drive away.

When I was on R&R, I would take trips in the country around Tokyo. It was a beautiful area. Most of downtown Tokyo had been fire bombed and was not an attractive sight. I went to Yokusuka where there were Buddhist temples, and I visited Donald Blackmon on a sea-plane tender in the navy.

The Japanese people were very kind and the most polite people. The general public were so hungry they would come to the hospital and eat out of the trash. Several of the young Japanese boys did odd jobs around my ward for food.

It was really a good experience, but I would not want to do it again. I was stationed at the hospital in Tokyo for thirteen months before being sent home. I arrived home in October 1946. I made many good friends and have kept in contact with some through the years. I am also eligible to get medical care from the Veteran's Out-Patient Clinic.

The thing I missed most while in the service was my family. I was from a very close family that included my parents, younger brother and sister, grandparents, uncles and aunts and cousins. I often received CARE packages from home.

—ERNEST DURRETT, *ABERNATHY*

Unforeseen Consequences

Many unintended tragedies occurred as the Native American cultures met the new, ambitious European forces. So it was with Spanish and French expeditions crossing the country that would be Texas. Expeditions, of course, don't last long, but their effects often do. The La Salle-Moscoso army, in their three-year trek from Florida through Texas to Mexico, spread smallpox among the Native American population so that in a year's time, two out of three Indians within trading distance along their route died. Thus it was with the **Loosing of the Spanish Horses**. When Francisco Vasquez de Coronado brought his clattering, clanging, dust-cloud-raising army through the Southwest in 1540–42, he littered his route with pots, pans, knives, armor, bullets, muskets, cart wheels, and every other piece of baggage and equipment that could be lost, broken, or discarded.

Even more than the curious pieces of steel, wood, leather, and fabric the army left strewn around, the indigenous folks of those regions appreciated the stray Spanish horses, which fascinated them. Add Coronado's horses to those lost by the Spanish settlements in New Mexico in the seventeenth century, and you can see that there must have been quite an infusion of this new technology into the indigenous cultures.

The formerly unmounted Indians of the central plains, mainly the **Comanches and Kiowas, quickly adopted the horse as an integral part of their culture.** With their new capability for reaching distant places, these Indians were the frontier equivalent of today's Stealth fighters. They terrorized both European and Native American settlements from present-day Kansas to deep into Tamaulipas and Coahuila in Mexico. And of course Texas was in the middle of this strike zone. Settlers didn't know the raiders were coming until they were gone.

The human consequences of these depredations are stunning even from our vantage point in the twenty-first century. During the eighteenth century, the Spanish were powerless to contend with them. Missions were decimated and

stock farmers murdered. During the nineteenth century, **the line of the frontier retreated whenever the army was called away.** One day in 1837, a band of Comanches heading home from one of their full-moon shopping trips to central Texas dropped in to visit Holland Coffee and his wife, Sophia, who ran a trading post in Grayson County on the Red River. The warriors' trade goods turned out to be one Mrs. Crawford and her children, whom they had obtained through uncivilized means at Bastrop, several hundred miles to the south. The Comanches really did like Coffee's stock of calico fabric and other doo-dads, so they swapped Mrs. Coffee (and presumably her kids) for four hundred yards of calico, plus some blankets and beads. Somewhat later, Coffee attempted to free a Mrs. John Horn in a similar fashion, but the Indians wouldn't trade. Maybe the calico market was saturated. At any rate, Mrs. Horn, who later gained her freedom, reported that Holland Coffee cried like a baby when the Comanches refused his offers. He gave her and her children clothes and flour and wished them well.

Miss Lee

Many people appear in history—especially in personal memoirs—for only a moment and then are silent. We wish we knew the rest of their stories. A young lady known to us only as **"Miss Lee" flashes like a spark into our view** and is gone before we get to know her. It is 1872 near Fort Griffin in North Texas. Indians have attacked the Lee family, killing four. They've taken three children with them: an eighteen-year-old girl, a girl about sixteen, and a boy about ten. It is the middle of May, and a company of Colonel Ranald Slidell Mackenzie's Fourth United States Cavalry is on its way to Fort Griffin. Henry Strong, a scout for the company, wrote the following many years later:

> The first night after the capture, the oldest girl, having been raised on
> the frontiers and prairies, understood courses and how to travel on the

prairie, and while the Indians were asleep she slipped away from them and followed the back trail by moonlight, and when we met her the second evening she thought we were Indians when she first saw us, and hid in a little washed out place in the prairie until she discovered that we were friends. She came toward us, throwing up her hands with joy. Gen. McKinzie *[sic]* sent her back, under escort, to Fort Griffin.

And that's all we know about Miss Lee. We wish her many years well-lived, even as we know that her time has long been spent.

The Gulf

Texas wouldn't be Texas without the Gulf of Mexico. It's by way of the Gulf that Spanish explorers came here, and by way of the Gulf that most European immigrants arrived. During the nineteenth century, supplies arrived by the Gulf from New Orleans, and passengers regularly traveled from Texas to Florida and around Florida to New York and Europe.

At 615,000 square miles, **the Gulf is more than twice the size of Texas.** Its average depth is 4,800 feet and its deepest part, a cleft called the Sigsbee Deep, is more than 12,000 feet deep. On land, a ribbon of coastal plain 50 to 100 miles wide parallels the shoreline. This plain slants toward the Gulf at about five feet per mile.

TEXAS AND MEXICO

Of course, Texas is not alone on the Gulf. Our neighbors on the mainland are:

The U.S. states of	And the Mexican states of
Florida	Tamaulipas
Alabama	Vera Cruz
Mississippi	Tabasco
Louisiana	Campeche
	Yucatán
	Quintana Roo

Long, thin barrier islands are arranged along most of the 600-mile Texas Gulf Coast. The islands are Padre, Mustang, San José, Matagorda, Follets, and Galveston. Padre is the longest at 113 miles. In fact, **Padre Island is the longest single barrier island in the world.** The islands are the latest versions of barriers that have come and gone through millions of years as the level of the ocean fell and rose in response to the process of glaciation. The present islands are about 5,000 years old.

At the end of the most recent Ice Age, 18,000 years ago, sea level was about 400 feet lower than today.

Because of the curve of the Texas coast and the way the tides strike this curve, sand and shells tend to move toward the center of Padre Island. The wind then blows the sand into the dunes, leaving behind seashells. The smaller shells on Little Shell Beach come from the north, while the large shells on Big Shell Beach originate farther south.

Slowly, Slowly, Sinking Slowly
The land around the San Jacinto Monument near Houston subsided six feet between 1900 and 1964. This sinking feeling was caused by pumping water,

oil, and gas out of the ground. The city quit pumping groundwater in 1960, and now gets its water from Lakes Livingston and Houston. But there's another problem that no one has found a solution to (and probably won't). The huge mud wedge the area rests on is naturally sliiiiiiiding into the Gulf of Mexico.

In earlier years, **the Gulf of Mexico was touted** as the Mediterranean Sea of the Americas, and Texas as the Italy of North America. If Texas was Italy, Galveston was Venice. Before the hurricane of 1900, splendid palaces built by barons of commerce affirmed the idea. Down on the docks, fishermen of Mediterranean extraction plumbed the Gulf for their ancestral delicacies—oysters, fish, and turtles.

Texas has twelve deep-draft ports, fifteen shallow-draft ports, and two ferries.

The Port of Corpus Christi is the sixth largest deepwater port in the U.S. The Corpus Christi Ship Channel is forty-five feet deep, while the Gulf Intracoastal Water Way is fifteen feet deep.

There's a **sailboat regatta** every Wednesday near Corpus Christi Marina. Every Winds Day. Be there.

Still Sailing?

Texas once entered into an alliance with Yucatán (on the opposite side of the Gulf of Mexico): the Texas Navy would defend Yucatán from Mexico for a fee of $8,000 per month. The agreement was signed in September 1841. The second president of the Texas Republic, Mirabeau Lamar, ordered the fleet, which was docked at Galveston, to sail for Yucatán, which it did on the thirteenth of December. However, Sam Houston (who had been out of office two years) was inaugurated for his second presidential term that same day. **Houston disagreed with most of what Lamar had done** in Houston's absence, and this deal with Yucatán was just terrible to Sam's way of thinking. Why, Texas couldn't even defend its own coast with its leaky little fleet of ships. So Houston ordered the fleet to return to port. By the time the message reached Galveston, the sails of the *Austin*, the *San Bernard*, and the *San Antonio* were out of sight. Commodore Edwin Ward Moore didn't get the message until March, and it was April before the *Austin* and *San Bernard* got back to Galveston. The *San Antonio* sailed to New Orleans for refitting. While the ship was lying off New Orleans, the crew mutinied, and United States officials subdued them. In September 1842, the ship again headed toward Yucatán, but was never seen again.

Spain's gift, a replica of Columbus's fleet, is located at Corpus Christi. You remember the names of the ships from elementary school. There's the *Niña, the Pinta*, and the . . . the . . . I said **you** remember them, not me. Fill in the blank. Help me out here.[2]

Also in Corpus you'll find the USS *Lexington*, **a modern aircraft carrier open to the public as a museum.** Known as the "Blue Ghost," the *Lexington* has a million square feet of deck. It's 980 feet long and 16 decks high, and provides a home for a fleet of vintage aircraft. The Texas State Aquarium, holding 400,000 gallons of water and 3,000 animals, is situated right next to the *Lexington*.

[2] Wouldn't you know it? Jean Blomquist, our copy editor for this fine tome, was first with the answer. Jean says Columbus's third ship was the *Santa Maria*. That's the way contests go. Some are rigged. Get it? Rigged? Sails? Oh well.

The battleship *Texas* is in permanent dock at Galveston. The *Texas* was the flagship for the D day invasion of France in World War II.

Each year, thousands of sport divers and scientists visit the coral reef colonies of the **Flower Garden Banks National Marine Sanctuary** 110 miles out of Galveston. The sanctuary, one of twelve national marine reservations, covers twelve square miles—seventy feet *under* the surface of the Gulf. The sanctuary, located on salt domes, is divided into three sections named the Eastern Bank, Western Bank, and Stetson Bank. Coral spawning occurs seven to ten days after the August full moon, coinciding with the highest water temperature of the year, 85 degrees F.

At Texas's Marine Development Center, one of the largest marine fish hatcheries in the world, red drum and spotted sea trout are induced to spawn eggs by controlling the water temperature and the duration and intensity of the lighting above the tanks. The fish move from 3,000-gallon spawning tanks to an incubation room, then on to the outside rearing ponds. Since its inception, the hatchery has released more than 200 million red drum fingerlings into Texas coastal waters.

Charter boating is big on the coast. The venues range from catered dinner cruises with entertainment to multiday fishing adventures. Most of the vessels are 33- to 50-footers with all the amenities of home, including heating and air conditioning. They're under command of licensed captains who operate out of

Port Aransas, Arroyo City, Port Isabel, South Padre Island, and other coastal towns. From Corpus Christi you might put out to Baffin Bay, Laguna Madre, Land Cut, Aransas Bay, Corpus Christi Bay, and Redfish Bay.

The *Scat Cat* and *Wharf Cat*, which are large excursion boats, are common sights around Port Aransas, operating out of Fisherman's Wharf.

The coast offers **saltwater fishing** of all types—deep-sea, jetty, surf, or near-shore. The list of fishy quarry includes:

amberjack	kingfish	pompano
barracuda	ling (cobia)	red snapper
dolphin	mackerel	sailfish
grouper	marlin	scamp

Some Fish and Their Seasons

Offshore fishing season for king mackerel, ling, dolphin, bonito, shark, and other surface fish is May through September.

Fishing season for billfish is the same as for offshore, with prime times being August and September.

Bay fishing season for drum and flounder is December through April.

Bay fishing season for redfish and speckled trout is year-round.

Bay fishing season for speckled trout, redfish, and flounder is year-round.

President Franklin D. Roosevelt liked to fish at Port Aransas. He signed a fish scale that hangs in the Tarpon Inn in Port Aransas. Guess the register was full. "Here, Mr. President, just sign the fish scale." I know, I know. It's a scale off the fish he caught, and it was customary to rip a scale off and tack it up there.

If your marine impulses turn to calmer activities, check out the **watch-the-animals tours.** There's a Dolphin Watch starting from Pier 19 in Galveston on Saturdays, and Sea Turtle Tours are every Tuesday, Thursday, and Saturday beginning behind Texas A&M University at Galveston. If you're lucky, you may see as many as 600 sea turtles, including the Kemp's Ridley Sea Turtle.

The Matagorda Island Lighthouse first cast its light upon the waters in 1852.

The tall ship *Elissa*, docked at Galveston, **has sailed during three centuries.** She was built in Scotland and launched in 1877. The Galveston Historical Foundation restored her, and she has been designated as a National Historic Landmark. Although *Elissa* has been around the world many times, these days she sails only on celebratory occasions, and then she stays within a few miles of shore.

Shipwrecks

Ships belonging to the French explorer **Robert René Robert Cavelier, Sieur de La Salle,** sank in Matagorda Bay in February 1685. The *La Belle* was found several years ago. Now, using aerial magnetic mapping, the Texas Historical Commission has located a wreck believed to be La Salle's flagship, *l'Aimable*. More than a million artifacts were recovered from *La Belle*, and *l'Aimable* is six times larger. Matagorda and Calhoun Counties adjoin the wreck sites.

The Gulf's Dark Side—Weather

If you take the Gulf, you also get the weather. Mostly, the Gulf provides what we require of our coasts: salt air, balmy weather, and great beaches. The payback comes when Mother Nature shows her dark side. That's when **hurricanes and tropical winds** endanger our shrimp fleet and drown our citrus crops in the

Rio Grande Valley. Hurricanes spawn tornadoes far inland and overload rivers and municipal drainage systems. Heavy rain after a recent hurricane caused the Rio Grande near Del Rio to flood, wiping out entire neighborhoods that had previously been safe from such storms. You'd think when you live 270 miles from the coast, you'd be safe.

Hurricanes alter the form of our coastline and the land behind it. Hurricanes aren't just wind and rain. Other factors within the storm system also affect us—like the height of the tide, the angle at which the storm strikes land, the height of the tide when the hurricane strikes, and how long the storm lasts. Storm forces destroy dunes and carry sediment from one place to another, and they're likely to tear channels through the barrier islands.

More hurricanes strike Texas on the northeast part of the coast, toward Louisiana, than on the southwest side toward Mexico. Strong winds flatten dunes, so **Texas dunes are higher toward the southwest part of the coast.** In addition, the climate is drier toward the southwest, resulting in less vegetation, which in turn allows the sand to blow into higher drifts.

The Unnamed 'Cane

Because of information restrictions during World War II, **a hurricane** that struck the Texas coast near Houston on July 27, 1943, **was never reported or named.** The few surviving records indicate that by today's standards it would have been designated a Category Three hurricane.[3] More than 65,000 claimants filed for losses, and more than $17 million dollars in destruction is estimated. The Nameless Wind destroyed warplanes at Ellington Field and

[3] The Saffir-Simpson Hurricane Scale ranks the destructive power of hurricanes on a scale of one to five, based on wind speed. A Category One hurricane produces winds from 74–95 miles per hour; Category Two, 96–110; Category Three, 111–130; Category Four, 131–155; and Category Five, greater than 155 miles per hour.

heavily damaged Metropolitan Airport (later the site of Hobby Airport), the Shell refinery at LaPorte, and the Humble Oil plant at Baytown. The destruction reduced the nation's ability to produce aviation fuel, which no one wanted the proprietors of the Japanese and German war machines to discover.

The worst disaster in American history was the hurricane that struck Galveston on September 8, 1900. The storm killed between 6,000 and 10,000 people and changed the future of the city. Before the storm, Galveston was filled with millionaires living a grand lifestyle among its opera houses and mansions. The city was the first in Texas to have electricity and boasted fifty miles of streetcar track. Nineteen foreign countries had built consulates there. The city never recovered from the storm.

Galveston had been a cotton-shipping center. After the great storm, two other factors combined with the storm damage to take away Galveston's leadership role: the boll weevil arrived to decimate the cotton crops, and the oil business became important. After the storm, Houston became the commercial hub for the coast and later a petrochemical giant, a stature it holds today.

Pine trees knocked down by the great hurricane were used to build **Friendswood Academy,** which graduated its first class in 1907. The building also served as the local church.

Falling Water

In 1868 a raiding party of Indians estimated at more than a thousand boiled down from the Plains and swept through the San Saba and Llano river country, driving away 25,000 cattle. Now, that country is filled with hills, trees, creeks, rivers, and high bluffs. In short, it's not really easy to drive one cow where you want it to go. What we have here is a cow-to-Indian ratio of 25-to-1, not quite as advantageous as the 22-to-1 student-to-teacher ratio recommended by our esteemed educators. So the question is, were the Indians able to keep their charges on task? Or had they driven off more than they could chew? Could you keep up with your part of 25,000 cattle on a dead run for 300 miles while being chased by several counties full of mad ranchers? Apparently this band of Comanches had neglected to conduct a feasibility study of this project. They must have been youngsters, for those with more experience would certainly have told them lack of time spent planning a task often leads to stress-associated complaints toward the end.

Another group of Indians thought Mrs. Alf Reeves of Mason County would make good barbecue. In this glimpse, a band of Indians is gathered around her front door trying to break it in. They are so sure of their prey that they don't try to keep the racket down. They're working hard on this door, when Mrs. Reeves, whom Alf has left alone with their babies, appears in her attic window. She looks down for a good while in a calculating fashion, then leans out and carefully pours boiling water onto the culprits. Surprise! Mrs. Reeves has put murder and mayhem to rout! It's a wonder she doesn't rush out and do them all in. It's obvious she could. But, like the good Christian woman she is, she lets them get on with their rather steep learning curve. When she was elderly, Mrs. Reeves liked to recall—while squeezing out some tears—that she had been "a lone helpless woman." Do I hear a chortle, dear Reader? Now, let's carry this character study a little farther: when Alf was home, who do you think bossed whom? And when Mama Reeves said "jump," do you think those little tykes just stood there?

Of course I would like to segue to architecture at this point, but since **Frank Lloyd Wright** built his Falling Water in Pennsylvania, I'll have to move on to weather. The **fallingest water** on the official record in Texas happened on August 4, 1978, at Albany, when 29.05 inches fell in 24 hours. Unofficially, Thrall holds the record, with 38.2 inches in 24 hours on September 9–10, 1921. Now for the unfallingest rain the state has never seen, we move to Wink of Winkler County. I understand that when Wink started the year 1956, it was located over next to Lousiana, but by the time the rain gauge recorded 1.76 (that's one-and seventy-six one-hundredths) inches for the entire year, Wink had blown over against the New Mexico state line. In Texas, when wind and a dry spell coincide, real estate moves around. Wink was Roy Orbison's hometown. He probably wrote a song about it. Or maybe not. Maybe he winked and missed it, while he was watching a Pretty Woman, Walking Down the Street . . .

Texas writer Dorothy Scarborough lived at Sweetwater and attended Baylor University, where she also taught. Dorothy characterized the West Texas wind as wild horses in her 1925 novel, *The Wind.*

> The winds were wild and free, and they were more powerful than human beings. Among the wild horses of the plains there would be now and then one fleet and strong and cunning, that could never be trapped by man, that had never felt the control of bridle, the sting of spur—a stallion that raced over the prairies at will, uncaptured and uncapturable; one with supernatural force and speed, so that no pursuer could ever come up with him; so cunning that no device could ever

snare him—a being of diabolic wisdom. One could hear his wild neigh-ing in the night, as he sped over the plains. One could fancy he saw his mane flying back, his hoofs striking fire even from the yielding sand, a satanic horse, for whom no man would ever be the match. Some thought him a ghost horse, imperishable. But now his shrill neighing is heard no more on the prairies by night, for man has driven him out. He has fled to other prairies, vast and fenceless, where man has not intruded, and now one knows him only in legend.

So the norther was a wild stallion that raced over the plains, mighty in power, cruel in spirit, more to be feared than man. One could hear his terrible neighings in the night, and fancy one saw him sweeping over the plains with his imperious mane flying backward and his fiery hoofs ready to trample one down.

In areas affected by drouth, populations shrink, trees die, cover vegetation dies off, and the soil blows away. Ranchers deplete their reserves buying feed for stock. Dry land farmers plant seed only to watch the seedlings wither. Land changes hands and changes family histories when it does.

Texas endured eight drouths between 1891 and 1951. The big one, the worst in 700 years, lasted from 1950 until February 1957. Only 10 of Texas's 254 coun-ties escaped being designated disaster areas. During 1952 the Texas monthly rainfall average was less than .05 inch. Lubbock did not receive even a trace of moisture the whole year. As I write this, Texas and Northern Mexico are endur-ing drouth conditions that may turn out to be worse than those of the fifties. It comes with the territory.

On January 7, 1886, weather in the Panhandle suddenly changed from warm and bright to cold and dark, beginning **the worst blizzard in the history** of the area. Cattle froze to death against the drift fences that had recently been built across the Panhandle to keep stock from moving south. The blizzard was the beginning of the end for many of the large Panhandle ranches, which never recovered from their huge losses. One herd was saved from a later blizzard when its owner rushed into the cold to cut his fences.

Men wore buffalo hocks for shoes during a blizzard in 1874. Henry Strong reported, "Skinned, with the hair inside and laced or tied over the toe, a buffalo hock does pretty well to keep out the weather, and doesn't fit so badly."

Overgrazing the land with livestock and plowing up the prairies had one consequence no one thought of or desired. Now the wind had something to spend its energy on: the loose soil.

Again, Dorothy Scarborough, in her novel, *The Wind*:

> And the sand was the weapon of the winds. It stung the face like bits of glass, it blinded the eyes; it seeped into the houses through closed windows and doors and through every crack and crevice, so that it might make the beds harsh to lie on, might make the food gritty to taste, the air stifling to breathe. It piled in drifts against any fence or obstruction, as deep as snow after a northern blizzard.

A five-hour unceasing roll of thunder that occurred in Karnes County on Friday night, June 25, 1999, is hereby designated the World Thunder Record. W.C. Reader reported the phenomenon in his column "Country Boy" in the *Countywide* newspaper. I haven't talked to a meteorologist about Mr. Reader's

observation, because it's pretty simple to figure out. Thunder is caused by lightning, so that bolt must have just stayed up there, looking for a place to land.

I remember those red drifts along a white windowsill and my silhouette on my pillow. I remember a car all silver on one side after coming through a sandstorm. There was sand, the blowing, grinding kind, and there was a dust storm, the fine, black, powdery kind that settled silently at night. When you got up the next morning you were greeted by an alien world, one in which snow was black.

While James Carter and Bud Turner were driving on the Salado road about a mile and a half from Belton, the other day, one of their horses was struck by lightning and instantly killed. The other horse was knocked down and paralyzed for some time. The young men were blinded by the flash and considerably but not seriously injured.

—Source: *Scurry County News,* July 11, 1895

The hottest it's been in recorded history in Texas is 120 degrees F., which was recorded in Seymour on August 12, 1936, and in Monahans on June 28, 1994. **The prize for coldest** is also a tie at -23 degrees F. at Tulia on February 12, 1899, and at Seminole on February 8, 1933.

Texas Towns Flattened, Flooded, or Fractured Since 1818

Texans and their institutions, it seems, suffer more than they should from violent weather. It's easy to forget this fact when we see the affected places after a

few years, when most of the scars are gone. Here are some Texas towns and **cities that have suffered major hits** from hurricanes, tornadoes, or floods.

Agua Dulce	Indianola	Port Arthur
Aransas Pass	Ingleside	Port Isabel
Bagdad	Jean Laffite's pirate	Port Lavaca
Bayside	encampment on	Port Mansfield
Brazoria	Galveston Island	Portland
Brownsville	Jefferson County	Quintana
Clarksville	Jourdanton	Robstown
Columbia	Key Allegro	Rockport
Corpus Christi	Lubbock	Sabine Lake
Del Rio	Lynchburg	Sabine Pass
Edroy	Matagorda	San Jacinto
El Paso	Mathis	Sandia
Freeport	New Braunfels	Seadrift
Fulton Beach	Odem	Sinton
Galveston	Orange County	Sweet Home
Galveston Island	Orange Grove	Taft
George West	Padre Island	Velasco
Gregory	Pearsall	Victoria
Harlingen	Pleasanton	
Houston	Port Aransas	

On April 7, 1900, rain fell for twenty-four hours in the tributaries of the Colorado River upstream from Austin, then a town of 20,000 people. Seven years earlier, Austin had built a dam of limestone and granite across the Colorado. It was the largest dam in the world spanning a major river. A wall of water 71 feet deep and a mile wide struck the 60-foot-high dam, and broke it. Austin replaced the dam, but the river took that one out too. Then the Lower Colorado River Authority (LCRA) began constructing a series of dams that would create Lakes Austin, Travis, Marble Falls, LBJ, Inks, and Buchanan. Waters still rise, but through careful monitoring and control, the Authority has greatly decreased the amount of damage during the ensuing high water flows.

Staying with Mawmaw and Pawpaw at Nine-Mile Camp

Nine-Mile Camp was nine miles from Ozona. There was a pumping station, a tank battery, and six or eight houses, all in a row. The front doors of the houses faced a pasture. There was no street, just a single long sidewalk that ran in front of all the houses. We made mud boots and walked on the sidewalk until we ran out of tracks, then we put on some more mud boots. If someone knocked on the front door, we knew it was a salesman, because nobody ever used the front door. When I stayed with Mawmaw and Pawpaw at Nine-Mile Camp, I got to go with Mawmaw when she took lunch to Pawpaw over at the pump house. I sat in a red wagon and Mawmaw gave me the plate to hold, and she pulled me down a trail that went up over a dirt dam and down between two oil tanks and then up and down over the other side of the dam. The pump house machinery was so loud you couldn't hear yourself talk. The men kept the pumping station so spotless they could have eaten off the floor, but they didn't. Since all the men in the camp worked together at the pumping station, the families were friends too. In the evenings the adults set up card tables out in front of the houses and played forty-two and moon and cards. We lay on blankets waiting for Cheeka to come down. We were scared to death of Cheeka. He was the man in the moon and he came down to get little kids. I've only met one other person who ever heard of Cheeka, and he was from an oil camp.

—KARON ELKINS TEAGUE, *AUSTIN*

Keeping Cool

The average Texan spends nearly $1,100 for electricity in a year, about $250 more than the national average. But we pay less per kilowatt hour than other Americans.

Have You Picked Out a Name Yet?

Nothing recalls home like the names of places. Texas is divided into 254 counties totaling 267,277 square miles of both land and water. As most of us were surprised to learn in third grade, these counties aren't just flat and plain like you see them on your highway map. Texas's counties have tens of thousands of named places within them. They've got rivers, canyons, draws, arroyos, forts, bayous, lakes, creeks, branches, mountains, hills, river junctions, passes, sand hills, parks, marshes, forests, woods, plains, cities, communities, and so on.

People of some twenty-nine ethnic and cultural backgrounds named our places. Among those groups were Native Americans, Spaniards, Mexicans, French, Anglos, African Americans, Germans, and Czechs. I tried counting just town names in Texas once and wore out at 8,048. People who really count have made it to 29,000 past and present communities. When I had nothing better to do, I conducted some advanced analysis and discovered that this latter figure amounts to an average of 114 towns per county (but of course most Texas counties have fewer, as does Loving County with its one and only town, Mentone). But given the vast tracts of Texas countryside, each town, if still existing and evenly spaced from its neighbors, would have nine square miles all to itself. Pretty lonesome.

If we measure Texas as we would a house, we find that it has 7,451,255,116,800 square feet. That first digit, the seven, is in the trillions place in case your eyes blurred. This mighty number translates to 41,396 square yards for each of us 20 million Texans. If each of us had to carpet our share at $21 per square yard, it would cost us $869,313 apiece. And if you've shopped for carpet lately, you know that's a factory price. All told, it would cost $17,386,261,939,200 to carpet Texas. But we're not going to do it. Somebody would just track it up, **probably your children and mine**, bless their oblivious hearts.

Many towns disappeared within a few years of their founding, as did hundreds of our East Texas sawmill towns—built by mill companies such as Kirby, Wier, and Temple during the sixty years after 1880. When the mills cut out, so did the populations—usually to similar towns deeper in the longleaf pine forests of East Texas. And some towns lasted, changing their names as the generations passed. The first settlers of today's **Zapata,** on the Rio Grande, called their community by the practical name of **Habitación.** Later it was known as **Carrizo,** then **Bellville.** In 1898, about a hundred and thirty years after its founding, it received its present name to honor **Colonel Antonio Zapata,** a local rancher and military leader who helped found the short-lived Republic of the Rio Grande, which began in 1839.

Other place names are preserved because **something amazing** happened there. The Alamo. San Jacinto. Goliad. Gonzales. Or because they're named after someone who did something unforgettable. Houston. Austin. Crockett. Travis. Bowie.

Settlers created place names informally, as they needed some way to differentiate their surroundings. Anytime a store, cotton gin, or sawmill went up, the place was fair game to be named after the owner. Then as more people moved to these places, the names became official. Thus there were at least two communities named Fowler's Store, one Fisher's Gin, and a Flanagan's Mills. There was even a community called Flintham's Tan Yard in Red River County.

Even when settlers got together and formally named their towns, there was little assurance the name hadn't already been used. We have a plethora of same-named places (but none *named* Plethora, one of the few exclusions). We've had at least twenty-four places named **Fairview,** half of which still exist. And six **Edens,** two of which are still with us. Texas has had at least twelve communities named **Lone Star.** Five are still with us—one each in the counties of Cherokee, Floyd, Kaufman, Lamar, and Morris. Of communities named **Concord,** seven of twelve still exist; **China Grove,** two of seven; **Africa,** one of one; **Beulah,** one of seven; **Macedonia,** none of five; **Six-Shooter Junction,** none of two; **Egypt,** three of six; **Bluff,** none of three; Echo, one of five; Echo, one of five. Echo, one of five.

Some of Us Got Mail

This many-name situation didn't cause a problem locally, but it did if and when the citizens tried to get the U.S. Postal Service to establish a post office. The postal department, of course, couldn't put up with duplicate names, so many **communities had to change their names if they wanted their mail.** Since the officials who named post offices appear not to have made a list of existing names available to the citizens, a back-and-forth guessing game often ensued. Sometimes the process was so frustrating that the citizens, after making three or four suggestions, let the postal people name their post office. Others, at their wit's end, picked names out of the air—literally. The "chairman" of a local post office committee in a little place in Mason County read the latest rejection letter from the U.S. Postal Service and looked into the heavens for help. "Air," he said, "I'll bet they haven't got one of them." And so there was Air, until it evaporated.

Still, not every place needed a post office, so locally produced names pro-liferated. The first store owner in a new railroad town might name the place after his hometown, his wife, daughter, son, mother, or the girl he left behind. Or others might call a place after the first occupant. George Littlefield bought the Spade Ranch, built a model town, and asked his niece to name it. She named it after her favorite uncle, of course. Littlefield. My only problem with this name is, they didn't rename it after me when I was born there. Couldn't they tell I was going to be famouser than George?

Name Games
The number of place names in Texas makes it fertile ground for name games. I'm not sure the peculiar alignments of names that follow have any deep social significance, but here are some that might occur to you if you're a smart aleck and drive around a lot. It's also not a bad game to play with children.

Texas has a Silver and a Goldsmith, but neither Gold nor Silversmith.

Good fortune must have been on our minds when we named Dinero, Royalty, Progreso, Prosper, Big Dollar, Dimebox, Old Dimebox, Cash, Price, Cost, and Cheapside.

We have **Best** in Reagan County and we once had **Best** in Hays County. The first Best, as usual, lasted better than the second Best.

We've still got **Latch** and **Key** (one of four Keys we've had on our chain) but we lost **Kid**d's Mill. We also lost **Lock** (in **Smith** County!).

We have both Yoakum and Yokum, and they're not far apart. But neither is in Yoakum County.

Caput, once near Seminole, really is.

We have a full pack of canines: Dog Ridge near Belton. Chihuahua in South Texas. Coyote Corner in Andrews County. Wolfe City in Hunt. We had eight towns named Fox, but they all slipped slyly away.

We had three Winstons and still have Churchill and two Londons, but both England and Britain left.

Democrat is the incumbent in Mills County, but where is Republican?

Texans are a frugiverous bunch, and we've named towns accordingly: Lemonville, Freestone, Pearland, Peach Creek, Fruit, Fruitdale, Fruitland, and Fruitvale.

Lick Skillet was in Fayette County, and Lickskillet was in Grayson.

If your kid were born in Cisco, would you name it the Cisco . . . ?

If you have more little Texans than you can keep up with, we have a Nursery for you, northwest of Victoria near the coast.

Even though we occasionally have high winds, our towns keep their body: Flat Foot, Black Ankle, Scratch Eye, Goatneck, Elbow, Tarheel, Back, and Monahans.

We've had three Scotts, one Fitzgerald, and one Zelda.

Our Bronte is named after the author of *Wuthering Heights*.

Marfa is named after the servant in Fyodor Dostoyevski's book *The Brothers Karamazov*.

As far as I know, Texas has never had a Mesolóngion, but at least one Texan has been there. John M. Allen, who was Galveston's first mayor and a United States marshal, was with Lord Byron when Byron died at the town of that name in Greece in 1824. Allen was also a veteran of the Battle of San Jacinto.

Es *verdad*. We have a True. We also have Grit. Near Mason. And John-Wayne's Smokehouse Restaurant in Houston.

Novice in Coleman County is 290 miles from Novice in Lamar County. Let's see. I guess the way we tell them apart is, one has no vices, while the other is nearer Notrees, which really has none, unless the Notreesians have planted some since I was through there in 1966. I hear that Notrees used to have a tree but they had to cut it down to build something. Just for the record, Notrees has plenty of mesquites, but until they reach a certain size they're brush.

Nueces or Neches?

If you come to Texas for a convention, you should bone up on the names of rivers, battles, towns, and heroes so you can find your way around your hotel—

for those will most likely be the names of your meeting rooms. In the Renaissance Hotel in Austin, for instance, where I am as I write this paragraph, the rooms are named Bosque, Brazos, Canadian, Colorado, Concho, Frio, Guadalupe, Nueces, Pecos, Sabine, San Antonio, San Marcos, Trinity, and Wedgewood—Wedgewood? I have no idea. Yes, I do. All but the last are names of Texas rivers. At first I'll bet they also had a Neches, but people kept going to the Neches when they should have been in the Nueces. Maybe the delegates to the Grapefruit Growers Convention were winding up in the Order of British Potters chapter meeting. So it makes sense. Do away with Neches and bring in . . . Wedgewood?

Many people get the names of those two Texas rivers mixed up: Nueces and Neches. Maybe I can help. Now pay attention. Neches is on the east. You can remember that if you look at the second letter. Don't get it mixed up with the third letter in the *other* river, Nueces. The *second* letter in *Neches* means *east*. Say that several times. The second letter in *Nueces* stands for "uther." The *uther* one. Now the word *uther* is your key to the whole thing. The "u" in uther is to the left of the "e." Nueces, the river with the "u," is on the left of Neches, the uther is on the right. Left is west, right is . . . let's see . . .

Not to change the subject, but did you know that all rivers west of the Trinity once had large populations of *Polyodon spathulas*? That's paddlefish. Distinguished by their long flat snouts, they are endangered throughout Texas.

An Excursion

Ladeeez and gentlemennn (sound of cracking knuckles)—for your **wordological entertainment** I will now exhibit **How to get to town by horse.** Ready? Pay attention. This paragraph goes at a gallop. The American Quarter Horse Association, whose headquarters are located in Amarillo, boasts a nationwide membership of 300,000. If I were boss over there, I'd call my offices the Quarter Horse Quarters. A few of you vegetarians might assume that the term "quarter horse" is used in the same way as "a quarter of beef." You know, you walk into the meat market and say "Gimme a quarter beef," or "Wrap me up a quarter horse." Makes some sense, doesn't it? Nope. Maybe in France or Belgium, or other uncivilized parts of the world. In Texas, "quarter horse" refers to that variety of *Equus equus* bred to run a quarter mile, the racing distance this breed has made all its own. Champion American Quarter Horses[4] run the quarter mile faster even than the great thoroughbred Secretariat ever ran a quarter mile. Reminds me of another quarter fact that's lodged in my brain. **Halfway, Texas,** is located halfway between **Olton** and **Plainview.** The **Quarterway Gin** is located halfway between **Halfway** and Plainview. Plainview is well named. Every town within four days travel was in plain view. Of course you already know that just north of Plainview is the Town without a Frown, **Happy,** which is about 500 miles from Smiley.

While we're on fractions, I ought to mention that we've had thirty-two Midways counting the Midway on Highway 84, west of Sweetwater, that boasted the Midway Drive-in Theatre and the Midway Motel. The score is, believe it or not, sixteen here and sixteen gone. Is the glass midway empty or midway full?

Would you rather live in Muckymuck, Quicksand, Earth, or Mudville?

---

[4] The first American quarter horse was produced at King Ranch in South Texas. The ranch also originated the Santa Gertrudis and King Ranch Santa Cruz cattle breeds. A Texas institution since the 1800s, the ranch covers 800,000 acres, and usually runs around 60,000 head of cattle and 300 quarter horses.

Have a Ditto, had a Mitto. Ding Dong is in Bell County. Zig Zag was in Medina County, but no longer. It zigged when it should have . . . where were we?

Can you name five three-letter Texas towns? Dot, Bly, Bob, Boy, and Boz. I cheated and looked on the list at the bottom of a big map.

We've never had a town name shorter than Uz, and only one of uz was there.

Had X-Ray and Exray in Erath County. Same place.

Our Teacup was in Kimble County, our Tea in Gonzales.

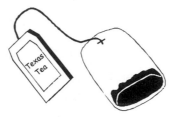

We've had forty-nine places that started their names with "Fort" and thirty-nine with "Camp."

All are absent where once these were: Ada, Ady, Aid, Air, Ard, Arp, Avo, and Ayr.

The town of **Agua Dulce,** Spanish for "sweet water," is located in Nueces County in South Texas. The town of **Sweetwater,** English for *"agua dulce,"* is in Nolan County on the Rolling Plains. While you're in that neck of the woods, remember that **Bitter Creek** flows into Lake Sweetwater. If your wagon breaks down out there, be sure to drink out of the lake.

Of course the citizens of Sour Lake aren't. They're as *dulce* as those in Sugar Hill.

Speaking of good taste, there's Chocolate Springs near Galveston.

If you're a real cut-up, you might like to visit Scissors (South Texas) and Cut (near Crockett). If you need a closer shave, then you ought to run by Razor in Lamar County or Gillett in Karnes.

Was Knute Rockne ever in Texas? Rockne got here, but Knute never did.

I deduced we had Watson and Sherlock by eliminating all the rest. What was left was elementary, my dear . . .

We have a Converse, but no Shoe. We had a Shoe String, but couldn't tie it down.

We have a Hughes and a Hefner. We need either a singular of the first or a plural of the second. Then we'll have plenty of . . . never *mind*.

We have a Medicine Mound and a Placedo. Something looks slightly wrong with that match, but I don't know what it could b.

We have a Sweeney, but no Todd.

We have Cotton and Schwab.

A Letter for My Family on Sister's 80th Birthday

I want to start my story as we were moving from San Saba to Post about 1919 or 1920. We were in covered wagons just like the pioneers. I guess that's what we were. There were no motels. I remember we stayed all night in a wagon yard. There were corrals to keep the livestock in and shelter over the wagon. There were several families camped there. Each one had a space to themselves. I remember a family that had two girls the same age as Bertha and Ora Lee. They played together and combed each other's long hair and braided it. A few days later they discovered they had head lice.

In Post we lived next door to Grandma Nicholson. Uncle Irvin lived with her and we got to visit with them a lot. Grandma passed away while we were living there. I remember after her funeral the house was so full of people that Bertha and I sat under the table to be out of the way. Claude was about six weeks old when we moved up north of Ralls. We were farming there. The first year I went to school, we went to Cone in a covered wagon. Hiley was twelve and he drove a pair of little mules. Mama would heat rocks to put close to our feet to keep us warm.

When we moved to Canyon Valley it was about eighteen miles to Ralls and twenty miles to Post, so we were really out in the country. Papa and some of us kids stayed most of the summer there and built our house then we moved in the fall. Living on that farm was good for us. We all learned how to work. We farmed with mules and horses. In summer we hoed cotton and made a big garden. In the fall we picked cotton. We had lots of livestock so there was always lots of chores.

We still had time to play. One of the highlights was to hike up to Tub Springs. There was a creek coming by our house. It was dry except when it rained. We would hike up that creek to the Caprock. There was a spring coming out of the cliff and the water ran across a large boulder. Someone had chipped out a bowl in the middle of this rock. It stayed full of very clear cold water and was sooo good. There were canyons and trees, a fun place to play. There were lots of wild plums and grapes there. We picked lots of them to can for pies and jelly.

Someone in the community would have a party and invite everyone. If just us kids went we would walk. One time we were walking up the road, almost home. It was real dark. All at once a rattlesnake began to rattle right in front of us. It was so dark we couldn't see it, but we went out around it and got home. Hiley lit a lantern and took a gun and went back trying to find it but it had moved on.

One time just before Christmas someone was having a dance, and the whole family went in the wagon. We had to go two or three miles and it was cloudy and cold. We had quilts and blankets and pillows to keep us warm. Just before we got there it began to snow. We had to take everything inside so it wouldn't get wet. We must have stayed till midnight and it was still snowing pretty hard. That ride home was so pretty. Everything was covered with snow. There was no wind and the snow was coming down so nice.

The family would go to town about twice a year—just before Christmas and once in the summer. Once when we were going home, it was almost dark and we were still a long way from home when it came up a thunderstorm. Papa just pulled in to a farm house. The people invited us to come in and stay all night. We didn't even know them, but that's the way people helped each other then.

There was a grocery store at Cap Rock. We bought staple groceries but we raised most all our food. Milk, butter, chickens, eggs, pork, beef, and always a big garden. Ground our cornmeal and made hominy. Always had a big watermelon patch. They began to get ripe, Hiley would put a wagon down in the patch and sleep there to keep the coyotes out. One time we had so many melons, Hiley took a wagon load to town and sold them for 25¢ each. They would weigh 30 to 40 pounds each.

Papa bought and sold livestock, and sometimes he would ship a boxcar-load of cattle on the train to Kansas City to sell them. They would have to drive the cattle to Post to put them on the train. One time he had to hold them in Post a couple days before he could get them on the train, so Hiley came on home. Papa had Ole Paint there, but he was going on the train so he just wrote a note and put it in the saddle bag, tied the reins to the saddle horn, and told Ole Paint to go home. It was twenty miles but he came home.

Our first car was a Model T Ford. I think it must have been

Hiley's car. He was the only one that could drive at first, but Papa couldn't stand that so he learned pretty soon. Next Papa bought a new Chevrolet. Him and Hiley were gone a lot so he let Bertha learn to drive so the family could go if he was not there.

Papa passed away in October 1932, three months before Zola was born. Hiley did the farming the first year then rented a farm close by the next year and Claude and Hubert did the farming. They were twelve and ten years old.

Hiley was married in November 1932, Bertha in December 1932. I was married October 1933 and Ora Lee in December 1934.

I feel that we were a happy family growing up. We were always very close and caring and we still are. I am so thankful for the loving caring relationship I can share with my sisters now. I'm so happy to be able to share in this happy celebration for Bertha's 80th birthday. I love you all very much.

—FLORENCE NICHOLSON MORGAN, *CLARENDEN*
SOURCE: THE FAMILY PAPERS OF PERNICIA SAVAGE DURRETT

A Preplanned Texas Tour

Guaranteed to PROVIDE THE TRAVELER with the GREATEST NUMBER OF MILES COVERED WHILE SEEMING TO MOVE AT A LEISURELY PACE. This very popular travel package was previously offered under the title HOW TO DRIVE SEVERAL THOUSAND MILES ALL IN TEXAS ALL IN ONE DAY. The customer should rest assured that the quality remains the same.

You may be familiar with units of measure such as the foot-pound, which is the height in number of feet times the number of pounds you lifted. We've developed a similar unit, based on another of the unique characteristics of gravity in the Lone Star State. This unit of measure is called a **Texas Town-Day**. Non-Texans are often confused because they don't know about this. In the normal world, from early until night, you could drive, oh, ten hours at fifty miles an hour average and you could cover about fifteen or sixteen inches on the map. But **Texas has so much gravity that it warps the usual qualities of the universe.** The exact mathematical formula is so complicated I can't devote space here to explain it, but here's the bottom line: One Texas Town-Day equals 9.5 regular days, give or take a few decimal places. Nowhere else in the known universe does a gravitational field exert such an influence. The Texas Town-Day is on the order of inverse symmetry in physics—you can turn a left-handed glove into a right-handed one by turning it inside out. A similar warping of space occurs during a Texas Town-Day. You have to experience this phenomenon to get an idea of how it works. So I planned a trip for you in Texas, from **Early** until it's time to say **Goodnight.** To wit:

If you start **Early** on a **Munday** in **May,** you can drive through **Dawn,** then visit in order **Sunrise, Sunray, Noonday, Sunset, Sundown, Rising Star, Star,** and then **Goodnight.** By the time you get to the end of this trip, your odometer will show that you traveled 4,058 miles and your watch will show an elapsed time of nine days and 31 minutes. The driving time was 72 hours, thirty

minutes. And you did it all in one day. Unbelievable, I know. That's what all non-Texans think the first time they drive here.

We have Lolita but neither Humbert nor Humbert.[5]

Texans have plenty of good attitudes to pick from. There's Joy, Splendora, Utopia, Smiley, Elysian Fields, and Mount Calm.

Friends Forever

Not all Friendships last forever. We've had fifteen, and ten of them are gone. Which reminds me. **Texas had a *train* called Friendship**. It was 1947. A columnist with the *Washington Post* suggested that the people of the United States should share their prosperity with the war-damaged citizens of Europe. Two months later, the United States sent seven hundred boxcar-loads of supplies to France and Italy.

States competed. Texas sent twenty-nine cars, including grapefruit juice from Brownsville, and three boxcars full of wheat and powdered milk from the Fort Worth Lions Clubs. The Amon G. Carter Foundation and the *Fort Worth Star-Telegram* sent fifteen boxcars of flour. Fort Worth set the national record for donations from a single city with eighteen boxcars.

The train that France sent back as a token of gratitude was called the *Merci*. It arrived at New York harbor aboard the ship *Magellen*, and consisted of forty-nine boxcars, one for each state and one to be divided by the District of Columbia and the Territory of Hawaii.

[5] Humbert Humbert is a character in Vladimir Nabokov's novel *Lolita*. I know you knew that.

The cars held personal gifts, handwritten letters, and one bridal gown for each state. Governor Beaufort Jester died before his order to find a bride to wear it could be carried out. The boxcar for Texas arrived in Austin; it is now at American Legion Post 76 in Austin. Italy made a movie *Thanks, America*, and sent **two golden horses** to stand on the bridge facing the Lincoln Memorial in Washington, D.C.

—Source: Exhibit of the Texas Memorial Museum

We have Rambo, near Texarkana, and Sylvester, near Abilene, but that Stallone fellow must be pretty Sly. I couldn't find him. We used to have a Rockyville and two places called Rocky, but I'm sorry to say, never a Balboa.

If you don't have anything to make up your mind about, drive over to Shelby County and you'll have a Choice.

We've lost all five of our Roys, but we've still got our two Rogers, one in Bell County, the other in Taylor.

They say never to mix religion and politics, and you know how well I follow orders, so here we go. We've got plenty of towns named like presidents: Washington, Jefferson, Taft, Roosevelt, Kennedy, Johnson City, Nixon, Reagan, and Carta Valley. And our towns have had a lot of religion: Angel City, Church, Christian, Lazarus, Little Flock, Moab, and Mount Zion.

We had Salome but only one Vale, and now it's gone too.

San Angelo is regionally known as Angelo or S'nanjlo.

In North Texas I find the town of Grapevine and the Grape Restaurant, but Raisin is a six-hour drive away, near the Gulf Coast. More sunshine in the south-

ern climes, you know. Get it? Climbs? Vines? Oh, well. I find that our pioneer aviator, Jacob Brodbeck, who beat the Wright Brothers into the air by forty years with a spring-powered airship, was a school master in the village of Grape Creek.

Dripping Springs, a town of a thousand in Hays County, is known to its residents as Drippin.

If you don't know why my favorite pair of towns is Wells and Teague, look on the cover. No, of *this book*. Good grief.

When in Texas, do as the . . . Well, we have Roma and Rhome but no Rome, Troy but no Helen (though Helena's close, it belongs to Montana, which we don't have either).

Speaking of Troy, have you ever noticed the artistic qualities of those perfect spiral passes thrown by the quarterback of the Dallas Cowboys? **Zoom. Pop.** Right there.

It's a place in Texas, but not a town: Maravillas. There's a magnificent canyon on the Rio Grande east of Big Bend with that name (don't you like the sound of it? *Maraveeas*), but no town. There's also no Quandary. Makes you *wonder,* doesn't it? But the Q's are well represented. There's Quail, Queen City, Quemado, Quinlan, and Quintano. Why isn't there a Quarrel or Quarry? Beats me. I *quit*. Hold on—that reminds me of Quitaque—pronounced kit-a-kway— set in a striking landscape just east of the Caprock in Briscoe County. Quitaque was named by the pioneer cattleman of the Panhandle, Charles Goodnight. Let's see. Q, Q. Oh, *yes*. There's Quitman, sounding like it looks. The *town* of Quitman is east of Dallas, six hundred miles from the Quitman Mountains near El Paso. If your Uncle George says to meet him at Quitman, that's different from meeting him *in* the Quitmans. It would be a shame to arrive ten hours late.

We have a Kirby but no Vacuum.

We have a Runaway Bay but no Bride, though we *do* have a Groom.

We have Olivia, Newton, and Johntown.

We have Pandora and a Boxelder. You figure it out.

Collingsworth County was named after James Collinsworth, a signer of the Texas Declaration of Independence—but the name was misspelled in the legislative papers that created the county in 1876. Lots of our other county names are misspelled too, but I figured you'd get tired of reading mistakes, especially since they're no longer misspelled, being a matter of record. Just makes you sick what they make legal these days, doesn't it?

It's Here—No, It's There

You can't ever figure out what I'm fixin' to tell you even if you've lived here all your life. A map will only confuse you. I'm looking at one now, and *I'm* confused. **About sixty of Texas's 254 counties have towns of the same name located within them.** About eighty other counties are (sob) separated from their same-named towns, sometimes by hundreds of miles and *have been all their lives* (double sob). You have to see this to believe it. Ready? I promise to make you holler and grab your buddy by the time we end this section, just like on a roller coaster. Are you game? Here we go.

Crockett isn't in Crockett County. It's 386 miles away in Houston County. I doubt that either David Crockett or Sam Houston would have approved of this arrangement. Our two heroes stood on opposite sides of the political spectrum, Sam aligning with Andrew Jackson, and Davy, not. Now to continue: following the pattern you've no doubt noted (or no note doubted), space city Houston isn't

in Houston County. It's in Harris. Here the trail temporarily ends, for alas, there is no town of Harris in Texas.

However, if my dear readers will allow an imaginative transition, we can jump from Harris to Paris, which isn't in France, and Ferris, which was no doubt named after a real wheel. Actually, it was. Ferris's namesake was Justus Wesley Ferris, one of those multifaceted individuals we find so often in the historical literature. He was an attorney, judge, newspaper editor, state legislator (he wrote some of the first Texas school law), banker, chairman of the state railroad committee, and, his resume just makes me tired.

Let's move on. Okay. Deep breath. Bowie's not in Bowie County, it's in Montague. This nonsense pauses again while we observe that, lo! Montague is the county seat of its own self. The towns of Travis and Reagan are in Falls County near Temple and Waco, whereas Travis County and Reagan County are nearly three hundred miles apart. Though there's a Falls County, there's no town named Falls, but there is Falls City in Karnes County, southeast of San Antonio, and there's Falls Creek, a tributary of the Colorado, which in its hurry to see the sea, falls off a cliff into Lake Buchanan.

Lake Palo Duro in the northern Panhandle is three counties from Palo Duro Canyon. The town of Santa Elena is in Starr County. Santa Elena Canyon is in Big Bend National Park. Scurry's not in Scurry County, it's in Kaufman. The *town* of Alamo is in Hidalgo County. Of course *alamos*, being cottonwood trees, are spread all over the state. *The* Alamo is in Bexar (pronounced Bare) County in downtown San Antonio. Historical note: Bexar started out as Béjar, then turned into Béxar, before becoming its present self. There's a Webb community in Tarrant County, and a Webb post office in Webb County.

Let's close with a quiet resolution. A major chord. Some names in Texas actually match. Frio Town is on the Frio River, Sabinal is on the Sabinal River, and Utopia is in, well utopia. It's beautiful there, green trees, fields, and quiet . . .

Excuse me. I was looking out an office window at the traffic. Back to our place piece. San Antonio is on the San Antonio River and Neches is pretty close

to the Neches, Trinity is on the Trinity. But the Angelina River has no Angelina. She was a striking and brilliant Indian maid who studied with the Spanish missionaries, then taught her people, but no one knows where she lies.

The town of Bremond is located in Robertson County, while the Bremond Block, an historical district, is eighty miles away in downtown Austin.

Clark and Kent are about 500 miles apart. Kent's not in Kent County. It's in Culberson County. Clark's on 146 between Liberty and Livingston. Let's see, at 250 miles per hour, it would only take an hour for the schizoduo to meet in the middle, at, say, Mason. So if we place a phone booth on the courthouse square, reckon we'd get to see the Flying One?

And with that, dear reader, we leave the subject of Texas's misplaced places.

Growing Up in Archer City

Mama Robertson, my grandmother, spent much of her time in the yard pulling weeds, tending the garden, raising chickens, and hanging clothes on the thirty-five-foot clothesline. She cooked every day—fried pies, Spanish rice, chicken and dumplings, and collard greens were my favorites. But the best of times in her home were in the evening when we would sit on the front porch; not sure what we did, only that I felt especially warm and secure as she and friends and family shared events of their life. As a child I was sure I would never leave Archer City, Texas, my hometown.

Approximately 2,500 people lived in Archer City, and I was related to many of them (the Robertsons, the Goodwins, the Malones, the Brays, the Forgeys, the Youngs, and the Jagers). Since mother was the last of twelve children, and five of her siblings lived in Archer City with their families, a lot of aunts and uncles were around to love and watch over us. We shared garden produce among the families. Mama Rob and my aunts would make me dresses and short sets out of print flour sacks. They knitted us mittens, and when these were wet, we would play in the snow with socks on our hands. We had two pairs of Buster Brown shoes: school shoes and church shoes. In the summer, when the school shoes were mostly worn out, we would get a pair of sandals.

In the summer, the neighborhood children played piggy wants a signal, leap frog, wood tag, hide-and-seek, and jacks. If we had

enough kids, we would play baseball in the lot back of Mama Rob's house. Sometimes we would just ride our bikes up and down the alley or streets. Down the alley from us, in the O'Keefe's backyard was a plum tree growing next to a shed. Phyllis, my neighbor, and I would climb the tree and lie on the shed's roof, eat plums, and discuss the mystery of boys. This was a highlight of summer days until Mr. O'Keefe complained to our parents.

Unless it rained, the only time Joe and I stayed in the house was on Saturday mornings when the *Squeaking Door* or *Let's Pretend* was on the radio. One afternoon I came in from playing, and my uncles and aunts were crying as they listened to the radio— President Roosevelt's death was being broadcast. This was a very sad time. We all wondered what would happen to our country without our beloved president, F. D. Roosevelt.

Mother played piano and organ at the First Christian Church, where Joe and I sat on the front pew every Sunday. (Mom could watch us there.) Our Sunday school teachers through the years were most likely kinfolk. Before Easter, Mother always bought me a dress to wear to church on Easter. The preachers were students from Texas Christian University and would leave our little church when they graduated. I'll always remember accepting Jesus as my savior in this church and being "dipped" in the church baptistery.

One day a stray dog wandered into our yard and gave birth to a litter of pups. Two of the pups were white, and my friend Jane and I got to keep these pups for our very own. We dressed them up, dyed them with food coloring, and took them walking in the evenings. When the rodeo came to town, we walked with them in the rodeo parade. My dog, Shortstop, grew up and did a real bad thing. He got in the neighbor's backyard and killed a chicken. The adults wanted to kill him because they said once a dog kills, they won't stop. I begged them to not kill Shortstop, so they said they would try something else. They tied the dead chicken around his neck and he had to drag it around for days. I couldn't even get near him for the foul smell. Finally they took it off, but this didn't cure him. They took him out of town to the country and let him out.

Our school was a three-story brick building with a band hall on the backside of the building and a gym in the middle of the first story. The bottom floor was for elementary school, the second level for junior high, and the third level for high school. The library was also on the third level. In the early days of my school career, the two recesses were the highlight of the day. This is when we would play baseball, have races, or play on the playground equipment. When the new principal announced that organized physical education classes would take the place of recess, I refused to participate, hid in the bathroom, and was eventually sent home. Mother did not take up for me and in a couple of days I went back to school and joined the P.E. class. I can't remember Mother ever going to school to complain. She played the piano for most of the events, including University Interscholastic League (UIL) band solo and ensemble contests. I joined the high school/junior high band in the fifth grade.

When we were in junior high school, Daddy gave Joe a car, an old Plymouth. The understanding was that Joe had to take me places too. We had more fun in that old car! When it got dark we would all play hide-and-seek in our old cars. Many a time Joe turned the lights off and we would pull up into a driveway and all duck below the windows as our friends looked for us. In my junior year at high school, Daddy bought a brand new Dodge. By this time, most of us could get our parents' cars and go "driving." We usually drove around the square; however, in the evenings we might go out to one of the new country roads and race. Two cars would line up on a two-lane highway and someone would yell "Get on your mark, get set, go!" and we would race to a designated stopping point—usually a tree. Daddy had a powerful car, and I always won the races. This was brought to an abrupt halt the day after I raced and beat Carl. Carl told his daddy about my racing and his daddy told my daddy. When asked, I had to tell the truth, and Daddy grounded me from driving the car for the entire year!

On the weekends, most of the girls would have slumber parties. We would sleep and eat on quilt pallets on the floor. Sometimes we would walk around town, singing or getting into minor mischief. But generally, we would eat, talk about boys, and tell ghost stories. Our dates consisted of going to a movie in Wichita Falls, going to a dance, riding around with another couple, getting a hamburger at the Wildcatter (the local drive-in) or going to a party at someone's house.

—ANNE NEEL, *AUSTIN*

Some Origins

Bandera, meaning "banner" or "flag" in Spanish, marked the boundary between Spanish and Indian hunting grounds. Battles between Spanish *conquistadores*, Apaches, and Comanches occurred at Bandera Pass.

Flatonia was named for F. W. Flato.

Henry Millard, commander of the right flank of the regular infantry of the Texas army at the Battle of San Jacinto, lived on to lay out the city of **Beaumont** and give it his wife's maiden name.

Mission, in Hidalgo County, was named after **La Lometa Mission chapel**, which was built by the Oblate Fathers, first in 1865, and rebuilt in 1899. The chapel served as their headquarters from 1865 to 1904.

During the 1880s one Ed Jones set up a store and stagecoach stop on Wanderer's Creek in Hardeman County. It's near where the Red River hits the Panhandle. He was from **Chillicothe,** Ohio. Guess what he named his spot?

Padre Island is the largest undeveloped barrier island in the continental United States, named after **Fr. Nicholas Balli,** a Spanish missionary who worked among the Karankawas, the same tribe that thought the first Spaniards had such good taste.

You're Here . . .

Texans came from most places in the United States and brought the names of their towns with them: Boston, Decatur, Detroit, Memphis, Miami (pronounced *Miama*), New York, Nome, Old Boston, Omaha, Pittsburg, Rhode Island, Rochester, Rock Island, Saginaw, Saint Jo, Saint Paul, Scranton, Selma, and Washington (on-the-Brazos). If you're visiting from over the big waters, you might like the Texas version of your town if you're from Bristol, Dublin, Liverpool, Nassau Bay, Nazareth, Odessa, Sidney, or Weimar. Of course, we have to have a few nations to go with all these cities, so we have Egypt, India, and Scotland, among others.

. . . and We're There

Ahem. **I would like to thank all our sister states** who make us Texans feel right at home by keeping familiar towns handy. We can visit **Dallas** in fourteen states: Alabama (2), Arkansas, Colorado, Florida, Georgia, Maine, Missouri, North Carolina, Oregon, Pennsylvania, South Dakota, Tennessee, West Virginia, and Wisconsin; **Houston** in nineteen: Alabama, Arkansas, Colorado, Delaware (2), Florida, Georgia, Idaho, Illinois, Indiana, Kentucky, Louisiana, Minnesota, Mississippi (2), Missouri, Nebraska, North Carolina (2), Ohio, Pennsylvania, and Tennessee. (And that's not counting Hughson, California.)

Sometimes, when we're away, we just really need to be **in the State of Texas,** and other states have accommodated us there too. Like roadside parks, communities called **Texas** are in Alabama, Georgia, Indiana, Kentucky, Louisiana, Maine, Maryland, Mississippi (2), New Jersey (2), New York (2). Ohio, Pennsylvania, South Carolina, and Vermont. Nevada has **Texas Acres** and Missouri has **Texas Bend.** Illinois has **Texas City** (as does Texas) and Pennsylvania has **Texas Corner.** Michigan has **Texas Corners** and Colorado has **Texas Creek** and Tennessee has **Texas Settlement.** There's a community called **Texans** in North Carolina, and one called **Texanna** in Oklahoma. New York has **Texas Valley** and Alabama has **Texasville.** Although Larry McMurtry's novel by that name takes place in Texas, we, in truth have no Texasville.

Sadly, there's no Texas, Texas. We get by with **Texline**, next to the New Mexico border and the town in Texas that is farthest northwest. We've also got **Texla, Texon,** and **Texroy.**

Being on state lines causes some schizophrenic names: **Texhoma** is in Texas and Oklahoma, **Texarkana** in Texas and Arkansas. While I'm treading water, there's a **Lake Texoma** without the H, and it's nowhere near the one with it. **Texhoma** is next to the Oklahoma Panhandle at the top of the Texas Panhandle, while the lake is miles away on the Red River border with Oklahoma (the wiggly part). If *schizo-* means *split into two parts*, then *trizo-* must mean into *three*. My nomination for most appropriately named **trizophrenic community** is **Three States,** at the point where the eastern border of Texas meets the southwest corner of Arkansas and the northwest corner of Louisiana.

Our Reno (northeast Texas) is between Detroit and Paris, and also near Sun Valley.

If you would like a Texas school named for you, it would help if you were the Father of Texas or died at the Alamo. Thirty-nine campuses are named after Stephen F. Austin, thirty-six after David Crockett, twenty-nine after William B. Travis, and twenty-seven after James Bowie. Another thirty-three are named for Mirabeau Buonaparte Lamar, the visionary second president of the Republic of Texas who set the Texas education system in motion. In addition, ten campuses are named after the Alamo, which itself was named after a cottonwood tree. If you happen to be a military hero, you also might have a chance. Nimitz Elementary School in Kerrville, Nimitz High School in Irving, Nimitz Junior High in Ector County, and Nimitz Middle School in North East Independent School District (ISD) are named after Admiral Chester Nimitz, legendary naval tactician of the Pacific. Admiral Nimitz grew up in the German Hill Country town of Fredericksburg, which maintains a museum in his honor in the hotel his father owned. An adjunct of this excellent museum is the Peace Garden, a gift of the Japanese people.

I like the sound of Flat, Zorn, and Rule.

Place names I like, just for their sounds: Bleiblerville, Bofecillos Mountains and Bofecillos Canyon, Brazos Santiago, Levelland, Mertzon.

Some of **my favorite places,** just because: Divot, Edcouch, Jot Em Down, Lazbuddie, Mutt and Jeff, and Tom Bean.

Is Rose City the Rose Capital of Texas? No. That's Tyler.

I can look on a Texas map and see some of my favorite plants: Evergreen, Nopal, Posey, Plum, Rosebud, and Rosevine.

The Time He Saved His Brother

Author's Note: Robert Caruthers, my mother's youngest brother, was crippled by polio in 1927 when he was twenty-four years old. Thereafter, he could not use his right arm. For a time he had to wear a brace to hold his head up. In spite of all, he carried on an active ranching life during the thirties and forties in the country around Barnhart and Ozona, usually in league with his brother, Abe, whom he loved beyond measure. Robert rode horses, branded cattle, sheared sheep, excelled at furniture making, and held any visitor transfixed with his stories and observations about the human condition. As I listened to him tell this story, I could tell it had stunned him, doing what he had to do. Here is the way Robert told it:

Abe and Louise and those two boys and me—this was when Abe Junior and Bob was little, back in the forties—decided we would go down on Devil's River and camp out a little. Spring lambing was over with and the weather was good, so we drove over there and set up camp. It was wild as a jungle then, and the most beautiful river on earth. That was before it all got to be broke up on private property. You could just set up camp anywhere you wanted to. Well, as soon as we got unloaded and the eats spread out and the cots put up, Abe wanted to go gigging for catfish. He had made

him a new gig, welded it and filed it down, and had it on a long
steel rod with a loop on the end to hold a rope. He sure wanted to
try that gig. He said, "Robert, there's catfish in that river that
nobody's ever even tried to get out." And there was. When we was
kids living in Sonora we would hear about the big cats that had torn
up trotlines. And we had seen them. The river in the big holes was
so clear you could see to the bottom, and if you sat real still you
could see them moving down in there. It looked like it was pieces
of the moss moving. It was all the same color, fish and moss. I
looked at that gig of his and I said, "Abe you aren't ever going to
get close enough to one of those old grandmamas in daylight to
gig her." But he'd shot grizzly bears in Canada and bighorn sheep
and javalinas and elk and now he wanted a big catfish. So he took
a tow sack and stuck it through his belt and he said, "Now Robert,
I'll meet you back here in about an hour and we'll see who's got
the fish." I worked my way down one way and Abe went the other.
After an hour or so I hadn't even got a bite. I figured I better start
back, so I worked the river all the way, and when I got to where we
started, Abe wasn't there. I thought it had been quite a bit more
than an hour, so I walked on up the way he had gone. I didn't see
him anywhere, and I just stopped and was looking around when I
saw that tow sack of his laying out on a rock pretty far out in the
water. I thought that was pretty damn strange so I hopped out on
the other rocks until I got to the sack. I was standing there looking
at it thinking, Now what the hell, when I saw Abe way down in that
water. He was hung up by his belt on a limb on a big tree that was

under there. He had tied the rope that was on that gig around his waist, and he had gigged a catfish and it had pulled him in, and he couldn't get loose from it. So I didn't even take my shoes off. I jumped in feet first and swum down to him. He had already given up. I didn't know how long he had been there. He was just hanging limp. I knew he had already drowned. I got ahold of his belt and pulled it loose and swum and yanked and got up to the top of that boulder, and I got up on it and then I pulled him out and put him face down. I pushed on him and lifted him up by the belt until the water run out of him. He coughed and some more of it run out and in a little while he come to. He got all right in a little bit. For the rest of his life he didn't mention it and I didn't either.

—ROBERT CARUTHERS, *MERTZON,* 1903-1967

Not Quite Wright

When I was in junior high school, I had heard of the towns of White Oak and White Deer. I'd heard of Whiteface, which was named after Hereford cattle, which have white faces. But Whiteface is right up the road, eighty miles from Hereford itself. When Hereford looks in the mirror does it see Whiteface? Anyway, one of my buddies always said before Thanksgiving and Christmas that he was going to White Rat to visit his grandmother. This was before I took a liking to maps. Through the years I met quite a few people from White Rat. But I just noticed here on my Texas Department of Transportation Official Travel Map that it's Whitewright. It was a rodentmentary misunderstanding.

Waka, **Wamba**, and **Warda**—sounds like triplet sisters, right? If so, they must have had a disagreement. Waka is in the north Panhandle, near Oklahoma. Wamba is in that far northeast corner near three other states: Arkansas, Louisiana, and Oklahoma.

That's it. Quit screaming. The name-game roller coaster is finished. **Have a snow cone.**

Texas Architecture

Owners of steamboats on the Mississippi River often named the rooms after states. The officers' cabin, being the largest, was the Texas. So the term 'texas' grew to designate the structure on the upper deck of a steamboat that houses the officers' quarters and pilothouse.

The Astrodome (officially the Harris County Domed Stadium) in Houston, which opened in 1965, was the first major, fully enclosed sports stadium any-where. Designed to be multifunctional, it accommodates many sports, includ-ing baseball, basketball, boxing, football, rodeos, and tennis. Astroturf, the

artificial covering so widely used around swimming pools and on decks, was developed for the Astrodome after the dome was painted to cut down on glare. This measure, necessary to allow baseball players to see the ball, diminished the light so much that the real grass died.

Many settlers in new territory established their homes by digging a hole into the side of a nice hill, and roofing it with brush, then sod, if any was available. Then they shored up the front with a stacked stone or log wall, hung some kind of door, and settled down to quiet, energy-efficient domesticity. I understand that one of their problems was making sure the neighbors kept up the standard.

One family was ensconced in their new dugout when, in the middle of the night, a storm struck. **Alerted by the sound of trickling water,** the father arose to light a lantern and stepped into a veritable flood. A prairie dog had dug his or her (I'm not sure about the division of labor in a prairie dog family) hole next to the wall of the dugout. In a moment the wall at the far end of the dugout gave way and out gushed a river of mud with its quite irritated occupant, Mr. or Ms. P. Dog.

Texas Courthouses

The county courthouses of Texas are, as a group, our greatest architectural treasures. Most were built during a grand design and construction period, from 1870 to 1910. They are resplendent in native stones of all different colors and some of the most outlandishly rococo columns, overhangs, soffits, turrets, dentils, gargoyles, and buttresses you've ever seen. Counties have expended great effort and funds to restore these grand places over the last few years, and to today's sensibilities, they look solid, enduring, and beautiful.

All the main roads came together at the courthouse square. If a traveler got lost, he could go to the courthouse and find signs identifying each of the roads.

The Hill County Courthouse in Hillsboro, a white limestone beauty with Corinthian columns, ornate dentils, mansard roofs, and a clock tower 70 feet tall, burned on New Year's Day in 1993. Hometown supporters, including superstar **Willie Nelson** (who grew up in Abbott, a few miles south), raised more than $10 million from grants, donations, and benefit concerts to pay for the restoration. **Governor George W. Bush** was on hand to rededicate the finished building on April 24, 1999.

In Sherwood

My favorite courthouse is retired. It's the little, old Irion County building in Sherwood, southwest of San Angelo. It's the second of three courthouses Irion County has built. This one was completed in 1901, when Sherwood was about fifteen years old. Architects call its style "Composite," with "Victorian massing and Romanesque details." It has four entrances under simple Roman arches, and on top a clock tower, or cupola, made out of wood sheathed in sheet iron. That makes it sound fancy, but it's not. Its façade is simple, its proportions solid, and it's quite a bit smaller than other courthouses of the period. In 1910 and 1911, the Kansas City, Mexico, and Orient Railway bypassed Sherwood because a bridge spanning Spring Creek would cost too much. The railroad built its track on the north side of the creek and the people of Sherwood watched the increasing pace of life pass them by.

Mertzon sprang up a few miles away on the proper side of the creek, and in 1936 voters passed the county seat to the newer town. The courthouse at

Sherwood was abandoned, and it became like a spinster aunt, one that you visit occasionally. When I was a child visiting my uncle, Robert Caruthers, who had a farm on Spring Creek, I always liked to visit Sherwood. My favorite building, besides the courthouse, was the wood-frame hotel whose stair steps to the second floor rooms were so shallow that guests who wore cowboy boots had to walk up sideways. Just try totin' your saddlebags up the stairs sideways sometime. Maybe they just left them on the horse.

Today the hotel is gone and most of the houses, but that fine old courthouse still stands serene. Recently I looked into the state historical records to find out more about it. I discovered that the county issued bonds in 1900 for $20,500 at 4 percent, payable over forty years to finance its construction, which was completed by the firm of Martin and Moodie from Comanche. They quarried the limestone less than a mile south of the courthouse site, and cut and dressed it on the spot. The builders paid attention to the job at hand, for they had it ready for occupancy on March 1, 1901.

The grounds were landscaped with grass, trees, and shrubs, and a fence was installed to keep the horses out. Outside the fence there were hitching posts and water troughs for horses. There were no gates through the fence. Instead, styles, or steps over the fence, allowed visitors access to the building and grounds. The building used wood stoves for heat and kerosene lamps for light.

On the first floor, two halls crossed in the center. The architects accommodated—with one room each—the county judge, county clerk, and sheriff. The treasurer and commissioners' court share a fourth room. In addition to its official functions, the courthouse and its grounds provided a pleasant space for community events such as political rallies, dances, weddings, and classes of various kinds. During warm weather, church groups held socials or suppers-on-the-ground, Easter egg hunts, and children's birthday parties. After the Sherwood Courthouse was abandoned in 1936, it was used by the local canning club, and as a Baptist church, a voting center, and a site for the Annual Sherwood Homecoming, which was inaugurated in 1957.

The Bishop's Palace

At the same time that farmers and ranchers were settling into their new dugouts in the Panhandle and Trans-Pecos, folks in longer-civilized areas were building their dream mansions from money they'd made in railroads and other ventures. In Galveston, for instance, **Colonel Walter Gresham (railroads) and his wife, Josephine, built a five-story palace that was so solid it withstood the great hurricane of 1900,** after which the Greshams opened it to hundreds of survivors. American Gothic in style, the palace was all stone, trimmed in blue granite from North Texas. Its roof was Spanish tile made in Baltimore; the staircase was built in Cincinnati and shipped down the Mississippi River. The chandeliers came from Venice, the damask wallpaper from London, and the marble for bathroom fixtures and fireplaces from Italy. One fireplace, made from onyx and silver for the music room, won a prize for artistic merit at the 1886 International Exposition before it was shipped on to Galveston. The Greshams had the palace's twenty-five rooms paneled in mahogany, black walnut, rosewood, oak, satinwood, and maple. They were known for their parties entertaining a thousand people. After the Colonel passed on, Josephine sold the palace to the diocese of Galveston. It became known then, as today, as the Bishop's Palace. When it was no longer used by the bishop, it was opened to tours. Located at Broadway and 14th Street, it's still a gem.

One of **my favorite buildings** is the Three-Cornered Filling Station in Snyder. It stands at the oblique angle formed by two streets. It's tiny, and perfectly fits the spot.

Presidio La Bahía, near Goliad, is considered by those who keep up with authentic architectural styles to be the world's finest (and the only one fully restored) example of a Spanish frontier fort.

What may be **the only outhouse** in the United States to receive a historical marker, the Victorian-style Arnold Outhouse, now owned by The Depot Museum in Henderson, was built in 1908 by John R. Arnold, a prominent lawyer. It's a three-holer with ironstone knobs on the potty lids, a Sears and Roebuck Catalog, and a bucket of lime. It also has a window for plenty of natural light (lawyers have to read all the time, you know), in addition to louvered shutters, doubled walls, and wainscoting.

Thanks, Mississippi

After renovating our prized state capitol building, the state couldn't put the new **statue of the Goddess of Liberty** back on the top of the dome with the Chinook helicopter they used to take the old one off. No visibility beneath. It was just too tricky trying to do it blind, especially with the windy gusts that are apt to whip around tall buildings. This situation was greatly embarrassing for a few days. Fortunately one of our neighbors—the Mississippi Army National Guard—came to our rescue. Using a Skycrane helicopter that provided the pilot a clear view, they flawlessly nestled the Goddess into her permanent position. This happened on June 14, 1986.

One of the more recognizable modern Texas buildings is **Pennzoil Place,** the twin thirty-story trapezoidal towers in downtown Houston. Designed by Phillip Johnson and John Burgee and built in 1976, the Place has twin eight-story lobbies roofed in glass, and a roof cut at a 45-degree angle.

Dallas Buildings

- **City Hall** was designed by I. M. Pei. Architect Pei also did the rhomboidal **Fountain Place,** which is sixty stories and boasts a computer-controlled water garden in its central plaza.
- **Infomart,** designed by Martin Growald, is a replica of London's 1851 **Crystal Palace** celebrating the Industrial Revolution.
- **Fair Park,** home of the Texas State Fair, covers 277 acres. It has been designated a National Historic Landmark. Check out the Tejas Warrior, an eleven-foot tall bronze sculpture by Allie Victoria Tennant, and murals by Carlo Alberto Ciampaglia.
- **John Neely Bryan's cabin** was built in 1843. The cabin housed the area's first courthouse, school, and post office. Bryan is considered the founder of Dallas.
- **NationsBank Plaza,** designed by J.P.J. Architects, Inc., is the world's 14th tallest building. It's outlined with two miles of green argon.
- **Thanks-Giving Square** was designed by Phillip Johnson.
- **Union Station,** a 1914 neoclassic gem, is now the Amtrak terminal.

Phillip Johnson also designed the Art Museum of South Texas. Architect Johnson developed a structure that allows fine views of Corpus Christi Bay among the exhibits.

St. Stanislaus Catholic Church in Bandera is the second oldest Polish Catholic Church in the U.S. In 1855 sixteen Polish families located at Bandera to make shingles from the cypress trees.

Sand Castles

Not all grand structures in Texas are built to last. On East Beach at Galveston in June 1999, seventy-five teams made up of architects, contractors, and others

in construction participated in the fourteenth **annual AIA Sandcastle Competition.** Using shovels, water pumps, wheelbarrows, and kitchen utensils, they constructed entries such as a Tasmanian Devil, a Sphinx with President Clinton's face, a San Jacinto Monument, a twelve-foot-high medieval village, and a real sand castle with a dragon. More than thirty thousand beachgoers strolled past. I'm told most of the folks involved in this activity have a lot of grit, at least by the time they leave.

Curandero of the People

Don Pedrito Jaramillo was the most universally respected *curandero* in Texas. He came to the Falfurrias area in 1881 to settle on the Los Olmos Ranch. He received his divine appointment after being knocked unconscious by a limb while riding alone far out in the brush. When he came to, he was bleeding from a severe gash across his nose. He packed his injury with mud from a a nearby streambed. Don Pedrito cared for himself in this way for two days, and then he slept. Deep in his sleep, a voice spoke to him informing him that he was now a healer by the power of God. Don Pedrito arose and went forth to help people who were in need. As word spread that he was indeed a true healer, throngs came to receive his cures. Don Pedrito did not claim credit for healing them. He said their own faith was responsible. He charged nothing for his services, asking instead that his followers help other people. He died in 1907 at age seventy-eight. Caretakers of his shrine north of Falfurrias estimate that 50,000 people come to visit each year.

Don Pedrito Jaramillo

El día cuatro de julio,
presente lo tengo yo,
que Pedrito Jaramillo
ese día se retiró,
ese dia se retiró.

Adiós, hermano Pedrito,
échanos tu bendición
a todos estos hermanos
que estamos en la reunión,
que estamos en la reunión.

Adiós, hermano Pedrito,
de la ciencia espiritual,
aquí nos quedamos tristes,
sabe Dios si volverás,
sabe Dios si volverás.

No se te olvide, Pedrito,
déjanos recomendado
a todos estos hermanos
que se encuentran a tu lado,
que se encuentran a tu lado.

Cuando viene amaneciendo
el corazón nos avisa
del hermanito que era,
el que ya se retiraba,
el que ya se retiraba.

No nos dejes, hermanito,
no nos dejes padecer,
ponnos en el corazón
lo que debemos de hacer,
lo que debemos de hacer.

A las tres de la mañana,
quedándome yo dormido,
oí una voz que decía:
—Adiós, hermanos queridos,
adiós, hermanos queridos.—

Pues ya te vas, hermanito,
a los aires extranjeros,
ya te vas a retirar
a los reinos de los cielos,
a los reinos de los cielos.

—Source: *A Texas-Mexican Cancionero,*
Américo Paredes, ed.,
University of Illinois Press, 1976

Don Pedrito Jaramillo

On the fourth of July,
I have it clear in my mind,
That Pedrito Jaramillo,
On that day he retired,
On that day he retired.

Good-bye, brother Pedrito,
Give us your blessing,
For all these brothers,
Who are here at this gathering,
Who are here at this gathering.

Good-bye, brother Pedrito,
You of the spiritual world,
Here we remain so sad,
God knows if you'll return,
God knows if you'll return.

Don't forget, Pedrito,
Show us the way
For all of us brothers
Assembled at your side,
Assembled at your side.

When it begins to dawn
Our hearts will let us know
Of our dear brother who was,
The one who is now retiring,
The one who is now retiring.

Don't leave us, dear brother,
Don't let us suffer,
Place in our hearts
That which we must do,
That which we must do.

At three in the morning,
As I was falling asleep,
I heard a voice that said:
"Good-bye, dear brothers,
Good-bye, dear brothers."

You're on your way now,
   dear brother,
To some foreign places,
You're now retiring
To that kingdom in the sky,
To that kingdom in the sky.

—Translated by Alvaro Guevara

Counter Plastic, Our Counter Plastic

Ralph Wilson, who founded Wilsonart International in Temple, built himself a home whose every surface—nearly—is covered with the product his company still makes by subjecting layers of melamine, resin, and kraft paper to high temperature and high pressure. This is the material most us are familiar with as covering for kitchen counters. Wilson's point was that plastic laminate is a perfect material for interior décor. Its bright colors never fade, and it never wears out. With revenues of nearly a billion dollars, Wilsonart has more than twice the market share of its competitor, Formica.

Gravitational Relativity As Generated by Magnetic Particles in the Brains of Texans

Gravity is different in Texas. I noticed it the first time I traveled in Iowa. I was watching the Iowa state map while my wife was driving. We were trying to get from Mount Pleasant in southeast Iowa to Mason City in the north part. I figured, looking at the map, that the trip would take pretty well all day. As we headed north on State Highway 218, I dozed, knowing it would be a couple of hours before we got to the intersection of Highway 92, which runs east and west. "Just keep going straight, I told my wife. I'll do the navigating." When I awoke we were passing through a town named Spring Valley, which did not appear on my map. This was not disturbing. In Texas, it is not unusual to drive through small communities that are not on the map. I looked at the Iowa map closely. Between our starting place and the intersection of Highway 92 there was not even an unnamed dot. Not long after this my wife said, "I never heard of a Rochester in Iowa, have you?"

"Me neither," I said, "Why?"

"Because we just came through it."

A few minutes later, shortly after lunch, we rolled into a gas station in Minneapolis, Minnesota, where I bought a new map. On the back of it, this map had, in addition to Minnesota, the surrounding several states including Iowa. We had started out at 6 A.M. and it was now only 12:15 P.M. We had overshot our mark by what looked to be about six hundred miles. It was completely weird. But we enjoyed Minnesota while we were there. We could drive all over the country up there and still be rested when we got back to our hotel.

This strangeness bothered me the rest of the two years we lived in the Midwest. I learned that other Texans had the same uneasy feeling, somewhat like car sickness, every time they took a trip of more than a couple of hours. Towns on the map just zipped by. You didn't even have time to decide what you thought about them. None of this made any sense until I read in *Scientific American* that scientists had discovered magnetite in the brains of homing pigeons. Apparently the magnetic particles are aligned with the direction of the earth's magnetic field at the time of hatching. When the pigeon strays from its place of origin, the particles swing toward magnetic north, and this winds a spring, causing a pounding headache and other physical upsets until the pigeon gets realigned. For the first time I had an explanation of why Texans' return trips are so much quicker than the trip out. It's the slingshot effect. The farther we get from Texas, the tighter this magnetite-powered spring winds. Finally, at about two thousand miles (the strength of the effect varies with how much magnetite we've inherited), we lose our hold on whatever last straw we've clutched, and suddenly, without even thinking about it, ZOOM!, we're heading back to Texas. My case proved the point. My stomach didn't settle until eight months later when I drove back into Texas. The instant I crossed the line out of Oklahoma, my headache eased as time slowed down. I kept check on my watch and my Official Texas Highway Map, the one with both the governor and his wife on it. It took me an hour to drive two inches on the map. Things were back to normal.

The Second Application of Einstein's General Theory

The first application, above, talks about time and space from the standpoint of a traveler. **The second application concerns the point of view of the observer.** Either way, Einstein's theory sometimes comes unraveled in Texas. The relativity of time and space are just different. Depending on your route, it can sometimes take several days to visit what you would think you could drive in a day. A nineteen-year-old sawmill worker named Dewayne Prescott once left Diboll in East Texas to take a load of planks to a buyer in Beaumont. He should have returned the next day, but he didn't. The town sent out a search party. They found no sign of Dewayne along the route. The buyer in Beaumont claimed the young man seemed to be in good health when he delivered the load. The buyer was highly pleased that the lumber had been delivered so quickly after he had placed the order. At first there was concern on the part of the management that Dewayne had absconded with the payment, which was in cash, but upon examining its accounts, discovered that the correct amount had been deposited in the company's Beaumont bank shortly after it was tendered.

Twenty-one years and a few months later, Marjorie Eubanks, who had been Marjorie Gifford when she'd gone out with Dewayne those many years ago, was watering her roses when she looked up to see a young man approaching who was the spitting image of Dewayne in the year he disappeared. He was looking at the buildings in a wondering way as he walked along. Marjorie was amazed. The young man was even wearing khakis, a red and green flannel shirt, and black suspenders, the same clothes that Dewayne had worn when he started his wagon and team out of the mill yard.

He drew up to her and Marjorie looked into . . . it was just amazing. His eyes, well, one was blue and the other was kind of an off-yellow. The yellow one drifted out to the side then homed in on her, just like . . . the real . . .

It *was* the real Dewayne. According to him, he had only been gone a couple of months. He'd gotten an offer that he couldn't turn down. It involved hauling some lumber from Beaumont to Corpus, and then when he got to Corpus, he got

another order to take to Austin, and while he was there some fellows wanted him to help them build onto a little ranch house, and while they were doing that, someone else . . . To make a long story short, this had gone on until his pockets were running over with money, and he'd decided it was time to come home. But he thought he must be in the wrong town (a lot of sawmill towns looked alike) because things just sure did look different. He gazed around him and asked Marjorie if this was Diboll, and she told him yes and then she told him who she was and he looked her up and down and just turned and walked back out of town the way he had come. No one ever figured out whether, if he walked backward along his route, he would unwind the gravitational relativity that had gripped him. It is one of the great mysteries of that part of the state. I'm not sure it's true. It could have been spread by boys who were gone longer than they were supposed to be. Or maybe it came from the girls, to strike fear into the hearts of young men who planned to be gone just a little while from their intendeds.

$$E=MC^2$$

Growing Up Bored in Uvalde

Looking back, it was the most wonderful place in the world to be growing up in the fifties and sixties, though at the time, we thought Uvalde was rather boring. Walking past the home of former Vice President John Nance Garner and occasionally delivering his newspaper was not nearly as interesting as hearing stories about Dale Evans and Dana Andrews from teachers who had had the good fortune to teach them, only to wind up with the misfortune of having to try to teach us. Raps on our knuckles and thumps to our heads were regular indicators of their frustrations. If they became really upset, it was not uncommon to see a chalkboard eraser fly across the room. Fortunately, I was as good at dodging as I was at disrupting class.

We muddled our way through somehow. We couldn't get into too much trouble, since sowing even minor wild oats led to being grounded. As small as Uvalde was in those days, if someone did something, everyone knew about it. The adults prided themselves with having looked after their neighbors' kids—though we thought of it as being "ratted on."

Television was new, and a few of us were able to fall in love with Annette on the *Mickey Mouse Club*, but the tube was not allowed to monopolize our lives. We rarely were allowed to watch as much in a week as the average kid does in one day these days. We spent our evenings cruising Main or Getty Streets. Each was about a mile long, and they converged in the middle of town. We would stop and chat over a soda at the Dairy Queen on the north end of Getty or over a cup of coffee at the greasy spoon (the name escapes me) on the east end of Main. Then we would repeat the process, until we neared our curfew at 10 P.M.

Perhaps the rural environment helped us survive the boredom. With the city limits no more than two miles from the center of town and three state streams—the Nueces, Leona, and Frio Rivers—less than twenty miles from there, much of our time was spent outdoors. Trips to one river or another were as common for us as mall-hopping is for today's big-city teenagers. The weather was warm through most of the year. December and January were the only months a few of us did not swim in the Nueces River. Most folks also skipped November and February, but not Tom Shockley, Dick Mitchell, and me.

We grew up with a great appreciation for the outdoors and while hunting was as common as swimming, we did not kill for fun, per se. It was just the way boys, and to some degree, girls, were raised in those days. Everyone had at least one gun—more likely several—and we were taught how to use them properly at an early age. Of course, we also did not waste anything we killed—if we did not eat it, our cats or dogs did. Most pickups came to town with a three-gun rack mounted in the cab window, typically containing a .30-30 for large varmints like coyotes or javelina, a .22 for smaller ones like skunks, and a shotgun for rattlesnakes or anything else needing dispatching.

Those pickups, by the way, posed an interesting problem for the U.S. Secret Service. When John Nance Garner finally passed away just shy of 100, the vice president of the United States came to his funeral. Needless to say, having to clear a town full of vehicles, each with its own mini-arsenal, was more than the Secret Service agents could handle. Finally, they just gave up and prayed.

Praying was an integral part of our lives too. Most of us attended church regularly, whether we were Protestant, Catholic, or other denomination. Some of us also regularly attended services with others in a manner based not so much on ecumenical ideology as on pure curiosity and friendship. Or, perhaps, because that was where a certain girl was a member.

Churches also were the main sponsors for our Boy Scout troops, and the Scouting movement was a rite of passage for most of us. Some of us even found Scouting to be a way of life. With a mom who later became the first woman to receive the Silver Fawn Award for her twenty-five years' service as a Cub Scout Den Mother, I had little choice. However, I also was fortunate enough to actually learn many of the lessons Lord Baden-Powell had in mind when he created Scouting. As a result, ultimately I was able to join the elite fraternity of those making it to Eagle Scout and Silver Explorer (an award that disappeared after my older brother and I received ours—reportedly the last two awarded). Summer Scout camp was an annual event for me, first as a camper and later as a staff member. Even during my last years of college when I also was employed full time, I used my vacation time to work a week or two every summer at Camp Fawcett, near Barksdale. Later, when my son entered Scouting, he was amazed I could recite both the Scout oath and laws—after soooo many years.

School has not been omitted intentionally in these reminiscences. It's just that getting an education was not my favorite pastime. However, playing trombone in the school band did become an obsession and, becoming first chair trombone, my ultimate challenge. While I was unable to unseat my best friend, Lou Fohn, I later realized it was only the result of his fifteen hours of practice a week and not due to any natural musical ability. Still, it had given me reason to exist, and the knowledge that perseverance pays off convinced me to become involved in other extracurricular activities—choir, speech, drama, the yearbook, and even track. By the time I graduated, I had made Texas All-State Choir singing bass, earned several first-place solo medals playing trombone, reached Region in Original Oration, acted in four intramural one-act plays, and performed in Region Band on both trombone and bassoon. Plus I was editor of our yearbook, *The Coyote*. That was the first year we used a likeness of the cartoon character Wyle E. Coyote in the yearbook. Even though the coyote was our school mascot, our advisor would not let me use the cartoon version unless we got permission from the copyright holder, which I told him I had got. That was a gamble, since written approval did not arrive until *after* the book went to press!

Alas, track awards eluded me, as my senior year I missed lettering by one place in the district mile run. However, I take some satisfaction in knowing that today I can outrun the man who placed just ahead of me that day—my long-time good friend from summer camp and current dean of the Texas Tech University School of Law, Frank Newton.

The voice work I did in drama, speech, and choir became the basis for my later career. Our local radio station, KVOU, hired a student every year or so to help out. During my junior year I was determined to be the next one hired. Owner Jay Harpole, after auditioning me, said I had talent, but too much "Texas" in my voice. Not one to quit, I spent many months practicing with a tape recorder and a microphone, "jist to git the twang" out of my voice. Finally, I wound up on the air.

Deciding to stick with it until I became a DJ was one of my better decisions. In those days only two places in town paid at least minimum wage—a whopping seventy-five cents an hour! The radio station was one; the other was the state highway department. The choice between hot, dirty, long hours as a road construction flagman and working as a disk jockey in an air-conditioned studio was easy. Plus, it was a skill I could take with me and use to pay my way through college, which I did.

By the time I was ready to graduate from Texas Tech with a degree in instrumental music education, I wasn't certain I wanted to be a band director. In discussing my quandary one day with a good friend named Wells Teague, he simply asked me what I enjoyed most in life. That's when I knew that I really wanted to stay in radio and television. So, while working on a master of arts degree in speech (radio/TV), I continued to work my way up through the ranks of public and commercial radio and television. When I completed my second degree, I was serving as a TV weatherman at KLBK-TV (Channel 13) and managing KLBK-FM radio station, both in Lubbock. This was fortunate, since I was able to avoid the Vietnam-era draft by converting that experience and my education into a navy commission. While my intent was to avoid Vietnam, that ultimately was where I wound up, albeit in Saigon as a navy public affairs officer working with the news media, rather than in the jungle working with "Charlie."

What started out as a three-year navy commitment turned into a twenty-year career. During that time I was able to see much of the world. For many years I packed my bag and headed off to Hong Kong, Australia, the Indian Ocean, Singapore, Thailand, and elsewhere as casually as we had headed to San Antonio, the Gulf Coast, or one of the Mexican border towns when I was a teenager in Uvalde. I married an army WAC from Rhode Island; our three children were born in Virginia, Japan, and Illinois. They attended schools in several states, as well as Japan and the Republic of the Philippines. Our "big city" living experiences and international experiences in the navy convinced my wife and me that we could never live in a town as small as Uvalde, so we settled in Dallas.

These days, as a retired Navy Commander and currently Director of News and Operations for the 150-station Texas State Network, with a wife of thirty years and three grown kids, I feel I have achieved some degree of success. I often look back at what's transpired since I started school in Uvalde in 1949. Scores of names escape me, but events and faces of thirty-five to fifty years ago remain vivid in my mind. They remind me that most of what I am today can be traced back to the solid upbringing I was so fortunate to have had in the small south Texas community known as Uvalde. My only regret is that my children never had the opportunity to grow up bored In Uvalde.

—JULIUS GRAW, *DALLAS*

Our Work Ethic

Texas has had six economic booms: land, railroad, cotton, sawmill, oil, and high technology.

In 1886 the work force of the Eylan sawmill went on strike, protesting their sixty-six-hour work week. They wanted to keep the same pay ($1.71 a day) but reduce the work hours to sixty. It seemed a novel idea, at the time, to work only sixty hours a week, and I don't know who won that strike.

Last year as I was fishing a tournament here at Lake Sam Rayburn, I hooked about a ten-pound black bass. I was trying to maneuver the boat so I could retrieve him from the brush. When I got to the fish, I reached down in the water to get him. Boy, was I surprised to see an alligator take him for lunch. Like to have lost my whole arm. That fish lunch cost me a $20,000 purse.

—Source: Glynn Durrett, Professional Bass Fisherman, Jasper

Sampler from the Karnes City Livestock Auction on June 26, 1999: 564 head of livestock were sold. Steers under 300 pounds went for $1.05 to $1.13 per pound. Heifers under 300 pounds went for 93 cents to $1.03 per pound. Stocker cows sold for $385 to $590 each. Cow/calf pairs sold for $585–760, calves for $40–125 each, while top hogs went for 29 cents a pound.

Computers

Dell Computer Company stock appreciated 88,000 percent in ten years. Dell stock was the best performer on the NASDAQ exchange during the 1990s. Michael Dell began his computer-construction enterprise in high school at Houston Memorial, where he helped fellow students upgrade their computers. Then in 1984 he was building computers in his dorm room at the University of Texas at Austin. The rest, as they say, was up. Dell Computer is now the No. 1 direct seller of personal computers. In 1998 the company paid its thirty-four-year-old chairman and CEO Michael Dell $109 million in salary, bonus, and stock options. Dell's compensation includes a salary of $844,231, a bonus of $2.6 million, other compensation of about $100,000, and 12.8 million stock options valued at $105 million. Those folks at Dell don't keep it all, either. In 1999, the employees pledged nearly $4 million to United Way charities. The company's five senior execs provided $30 million to help families with no health insurance, educate children, and promote the arts. The employees regularly volunteer at such worthwhile events as the Special Olympics. I've seen 'em there.

Texas added more high-tech jobs—101,737—between 1990 and 1997 than any other state. Texas is second (with 375,933) in the total number of high-tech workers.

Overachievers

It seems that Texas has had more than its share of people who did more than seems humanly possible. You run across them all the time in the 1800s when there was plenty of opportunity. **Meet James Collinsworth,** born in Tennessee in 1806:

At twenty, he began to practice law.

At twenty-eight, he was district attorney for the Western District of Tennessee.

At twenty-nine, he headed for Mexican Texas, where, at Brazoria, he joined the War Party.

At thirty, in 1836, he accomplished the following:

- nominated Sam Houston for commander-in-chief of the Texas Army
- joined the Texas Army, became aide-de-camp for Sam Houston
- received commendation for his actions in the Battle of San Jacinto
- served as acting secretary of state for Texas
- was appointed commissioner to the United States
- met with U.S. President Andrew Jackson
- declined appointment to be attorney general of the Republic of Texas
- was elected senator to Texas's First Congress
- was elected chief justice of the new Texas Supreme Court
- helped organize the Texas Railroad, Navigation, and Banking Company
- was elected first secretary of Holland Masonic Lodge at Brazoria

In 1837 he helped found the town of Richmond and the Philosophical Society of Texas. Then James Collinsworth died, at age thirty-two.

Pearl Payne

I was one of a set of triplets born in 1927. We were raised in a community in southern Oklahoma with all our cousins. Mother was a hard-working person. We didn't think anybody owed us anything. She always made sure our shoes looked nice and that we had clean underwear. Mother died in 1993 at ninety-eight. At the time she was in the *Guinness Book of World Records* as the oldest mother of surviving triplets.

One year there were thirteen of us cousins in first grade through eighth. We went to school at Four Mile and Trail and then when it was time for high school we went to Bray, Oklahoma. We loved to wave at the engineers on the trains. It was good luck to have a penny that had been mashed by a train.

We moved to Texas from Oklahoma in 1943 when I was fifteen. We came to Knox City to pull cotton one year, and that was the first time we had been away from the house. And that was the first time we ever saw a black person. There was a black family there pulling cotton and they were from Rosebud, Texas. The first few times we saw them, we run. Then before long we were friends and eating meals together. There was five or six kids about our age. They could sing. We were staying in a house that belonged to the man who owned the land. No one I knew had a piano at home, though there was one at school. So this family would bring their rub boards and guitar and other things they used as instruments, and they would sing and dance. They would sing "Old Joe Clark." There was always a caller.

It was a novelty to live in town. When we moved to Abernathy I got a job in Gertrude Prather's cafe washing dishes. We served breakfast and plate lunches and hamburgers. For our plate lunches, you had a choice of chicken, chicken-fried steak, or roast beef. And we always had two vegetables and coconut pie.

Ed Graham bought Gertrude out in 1949 or '50. He was a baker. I worked for him about twenty-five years. When the tornado hit Hale Center[6] we spent all our time making up sandwiches to send up to the relief workers. Ed would load up a van and take it up there. We sent breakfast and coffee and sandwiches. I never did go up there to serve the food because I had to stay here and get it ready. People in Abernathy are the best. You may not even know you have friends until you need them. Then here they come.

I've been to California. We went to Disneyland, and Knott's Berry Farm. I like to go to Post to the Old Mill Days. I was an oil painter. I gave them to my kids. When they started putting them under the bed I quit giving them to them.

My brother's house blew away in Plainview a number of years ago.

My grandson works for Dell Computers. He's given me two computers, and I don't know what to do with either one of them. He's a great big old tall boy.

—PEARL PAYNE, *ABERNATHY*

[6] The tornado that struck Hale Center on June 2, 1965, wiped out most of the downtown area, including the city hall and fire station. Five residents lost their lives. Damage was estimated at $8 million. The population is usually around 2,000.

Just Don't Stick It Underneath Your Chair

We have three Gum Springs, one each in Rusk, Cass, and Harrison counties. Of course everyone knows about Gum Grove. Your jaw is automatically moving, right? Well, chew on this—**Justus J. Schott** (1846–1928), who founded the J. J. Schott Drug Company in Galveston at the tender age of twenty-one, added sugar and flavoring to chicle, the thickened juice of a sapodilla tree *(Stickymas gumdaworksup)* in the hopes of making a new medicine. His product didn't cure any ills, but people started chewing it instead of the paraffin-juniper sap mix they'd been stuck with. Schott made up pamphlets advertising his invention, and for several years shipped quite a lot of it around the state. Then the Adams Chewing Gum company fired a schott across Schott's prow. They sued him for $50,000 for violating their patent. This was a sticky question, but our Schott was equal to the challenge. He brought his pamphlets to court and proved he had been making chewing gum for years longer than the chewing gum company. He won the case, but it left a bad taste. Schott became interested in distributing in Texas a carbonated drink called Moxie that was popular in the northern United States. He found he needed **a lot of Moxie** to fill his orders, so he started manufacturing it. Our hero soon stretched his manufacturing operations into one of the largest in Galveston. Mr. Schott lived to the well-fizzed age of eighty-two, and was buried at Halletsville, not Galveston, and I don't know why.

Oil Booms

Before we get to the booms, let's start with a no-boom—with a gentleman who was in the right place long before the right time. **In 1866 Lyne Taliaferro**

Barret drilled the first producing oil well in Texas. But no one quite knew what to do with the greasy stuff. The Barret well was in Nacogdoches County at Oil Springs, and it was only 106 feet deep.

Spindletop, 1901

The Texas oil business began in Beaumont on January 10, 1901, at 10:30 in the morning when Captain Anthony F. Lucas brought in the first great American gusher, Spindletop. This one event catapulted a horse-and-wagon culture into one based on petroleum. Within twenty years, automobiles, airplanes, highways, improved railroads, marine shipping, and mass production had transformed the world.

Daisy Bradford Number 3, 1930

In 1927 **Columbus M. "Dad" Joiner,** who had made and lost several fortunes exploring for oil, started his now famous search for oil in Rusk County, where geologists, after thorough studies, said there was none. Dad was broke, and had no equipment—just his overriding instinct that told him oil was down there. He patched together enough parts to drill his first well, and when it was dry, he drilled another, more than twice as deep, to 2,418 feet. Still, nothing promising showed in his drill cores. He had to finance the third well by giving up many of his remaining oil leases.

Dad sited the new location only three hundred feet from the first abandoned one, and set up his drilling rig. He drilled past the depth of his earlier efforts, and approached 3,000 feet. Still no oil. But neither Dad nor his crew would stop. They no longer cared that other oil people might think they were daft. His crew worked without pay, firing the boiler with wood from local pine trees. They held their equipment together any way they could, with baling wire being their main fix-all.

Dad drilled on, penetrating the Rusk County farm land more than a thousand feet deeper than he'd gone for the previous well. His ramshackle machinery groaned, clattered, and shuttered. Then, on September 3, 1930, the drill core came up dripping with petroleum from the Woodbine Sand strata. Dad Joiner had discovered the East Texas Oil Field, which proved to be the world's largest known deposit. The Daisy Bradford, when brought in, produced 300 barrels a day from a depth of 3,592 feet, and inaugurated the East Texas Oil Boom, similar in frenzy—this was during the Great Depression—to the California Gold Rush eighty-one years before. Covering 130,000 acres, the field is 43 miles long and 10 miles wide.

Just so you'll be reminded of these earth-shaking events, the folks in Rusk County have set up oil derricks over the picnic tables at Pioneer Park west of Henderson, just south of the farm where Dad Joiner brought in Daisy Bradford Number 3. And there's a monument to Joe Roughneck, containing a time capsule to be opened in 2056. So, if you're in the vicinity then, drop by and satisfy your curi-**oil**-isty.

Salt domes are integral to the geology of the Texas petroleum deposits. Most are underground or under the Gulf of Mexico, but six salt domes are visible at the surface in Texas: one near Damon, one near High Island east of Galveston Bay, and four near Palestine.

More geologists live in Houston than in any other city in the world.

The Permian Basin is the largest inland petrochemical complex in the United States, with its businesses centered in Midland and Odessa.

In the twenty-five years between 1948 and 1973, **the Scurry County Canyon Reef oil fields** produced one billion barrels of oil. At the billionth-barrel celebration, a petroleum engineer estimated that the field had made an average of

$225 per minute all that time, at $3 a barrel. Let's see, just figuring in my head, that's $43.5 million short of $3 billion. So I guess a little went for PR and a little for snacks and a little for the picture show.

Oil companies wanted the schools in the boomtowns to be the best. Sometimes the numbers of school-age children would grow from a hundred or so at the end of one term to a thousand or more at the beginning of the next. Or sometimes the increase happened within a few days as word spread of new oil activity. Invariably, this sort of growth put the panic on local school boards. Sometimes the school district's board of trustees summoned representatives from the biggest oil companies to a meeting and informed them of the crisis. Usually the oil companies stepped up to the line. In one meeting in Snyder, representatives wrote checks totaling $150,000 then and there to get the school year started. Whole communities contributed to the effort. Churches made facilities available for classes, volunteers helped the overworked teachers, and old cowhands signed on to drive school buses.

Wildcatters discovered oil at McCamey, in Upton County, in 1925. The town boomed, reaching a population of 10,000 practically overnight. But McCamey was a long way from a refinery. In 1928 the Shell Oil Company built a concrete-lined, earthen storage tank to hold the surplus oil until pipelines could be built to transport oil to refineries near Houston. It held a million barrels of oil, but not for long. The oil was so heavy it cracked the limestone substrata, and the tank leaked. It made no sense to anyone to put the oil back where they found it, so Shell gave up on the Great Tank after a year.

Few Beards

Down in the oil patch, workers in oil-well service companies don't wear beards because they might have to put on a gas mask to protect themselves from hydrogen sulfate.

During the boom years of the East Texas Oil Field, Gaston Independent School District was the largest rural school district in the world.

Segments of the oil business:
> searching
> > financing
> > > producing
> > > > refining
> > > > > shipping
> > > > > > pipelining
> > > > > > > supplying
> > > > > > > > marketing

Texan Howard Hughes, who parleyed the wealth inherited from his father's oil-drilling-bit business into a major fortune, once received a check for $546,549,171 (for his 75 percent share of TransWorld Airlines).

Man, Camouflaged

In northeast Texas, the small-town men have to hunt and fish. You open up a man's closet and it's all camouflage. And they have to have a hunting lease. It's best if the lease is in East Texas. Some of them, if they have a lease out in West Texas, they're not considered really a part of the group. The men, they love those turkey camps, and squirrel camps, and deer camps. At a squirrel camp they shoot squirrels and fry the breasts. The last week of camp, the women go out and they have a good time, but the women aren't allowed before that.

—KATHY ALLEN, *OMAHA, TEXAS*

Some Things You Can't Do Without

Southwest Austin, where I live, is thoroughly suburbanized. What used to be a simple two-lane pavement to Oak Hill and Dripping Springs, with a clutter of businesses like used car lots and feed stores on both sides, has become one of those highway interchanges that took ten years to plan, five to build, and was overcrowded the day it opened. As soon as the first stage opened, here came a Target and a Home Depot and an Office Max and a Marie Callenders and a Wendy's and a Garden Ridge and a Burger King. Wal-Mart opened a store next to the Burger King.

Early one morning I turned in beside the Burger King and drove on into the Wal-Mart parking lot where, among the yuppie Mazda sedans and big Lincoln Navigators, I noticed an eight- or ten-year-old Ford pickup that had a bale of dry alfalfa hay in the back, along with the makings of an electric fence. Several decals on the back window caught my attention:

Washington, It Ain't Your Money
Luckenbach, Texas
Texas Trophy Hunters Association
International Game Fish Association
University of Houston

In addition, there was a sticker that had a "DS" with a paw print—it turned out to be the Dripping Springs school logo. The owner walked up. He was thin, clean shaven, and about five eleven. He wore boot-cut Wranglers that were slightly muddy around the cuffs, worn brown ropers cracked across the arches, a plaid flannel shirt, a wide belt with a good-sized buckle, and a John Deere cap. He looked mildly excited, as if he wanted to get on with something before it got too late. He was carrying two boxes of twelve-gauge shotgun shells and a new (free) Texas Parks & Wildlife Hunting and Fishing Guide he'd picked up inside.

If you want to talk about pickups, you don't have to introduce yourself. Now, you're in a slight bit of danger if you're too close to a man's pickup when he

notices you, and the best thing you can say is, "I was just noticing your pickup." You don't prop your foot on his bumper until you determine whether the hair has laid back down on his neck. It helps if you're sincerely interested in his pickup, which I was. I always like to know if a Ford pickup has had more than one engine, and if so, how many miles he got out of the first one or two. This old boy wasn't defensive. He was the kind of guy who is so sure of himself that he's relaxed. After complimenting him on being from Dripping Springs, saying what a nice kind of country I thought it was out there, I asked him if he thought SUVs were going to replace pickups. He contemplated the ramifications of this question for the time it took to reach behind him and put his sack on the seat, then allowed the following:

> In order to carry everything you need, like your sacks of corn for deer feed, your dog kennel, your tow chain, your shovel, your circle saw, your hammer and nails for fixing the deer blind, your bedroll, your fishing rod and tackle boxes, and your tent and bedroll, you generally need to get yourself a pickup. Sport-utility vehicles are getting to be stylish, but you don't want to go throwing your chain saw or your deer carcass in one of them. And you tear up the upholstery trying to slide a trolling motor in between the seats. You need that metal bed you get with a pickup, preferably with a fiberglass liner so when you wear it out you can put another one in in just a little bit. And of course that tailgate helps too. You can let it down so you don't have to lift your stuff so high, and you can set on it when you're tired out and eat your lunch and get a drink out of your own water can. It don't hurt to get mud in it because you can just take all your equipment out and turn the hose on it. If you put yourself a side-to-side toolbox up next to the cab then you have a place you can keep your gloves handy and your socket set and your Crescent wrench dry so's they don't rust. So I would say that no, your pickup is going to be around for a good while.

As he finished with this master class, the man's wife walked up with six seventy-five-cent pots of peppermint dianthus from the Wal-Mart nursery. She looked a little better fed than he did, but she was just as friendly. She called him "Darrell Baby" and smooched him under the chin as if she hadn't seen him in a week. Darrell told her I wanted to know about SUVs and she brightened up. She said she would take one any day somebody wanted to give her one, but she thought they were overpriced and not very practical. "Around town you can't park one of the durn things," she said, "and out in the country you don't want to go driving it through the mesquite, them thorns will tear that pretty finish right up. You're used to scratching the finish off a pickup, but it would hurt to do it to one of those fancy things. Our horses too. They like to chew on chrome. Law, if I drove one of them SUVs out to feed, Darrell's old black horse would have the chrome stripped off in no time."

She laughed and looked at Darrell, and Darrell said, "That's the durn truth." She was leaning on Darrell and he was leaning on the pickup and he gave her a squeeze around the shoulders and they both said they had to get going. He went around to drive and she climbed up on her side and slid across the bench seat up against him, and that was the way they were as they headed back to Dripping Springs, or beyond.

From White Deer, Texas, to the World

I worked and traveled all over the world, but I grew up in White Deer, Texas, up by Amarillo. When I was in high school, we traveled to Fort Worth to a track meet. The most interesting thing we did was ride the escalators in the department stores. We had to drive quite a distance to get anywhere.

Then one Thanksgiving, my mother, sister, cousin, and I were driving home from my uncle's house in Amarillo. Dad called to tell us to stay there because a storm was on the way, but we had already left. Sure enough, after dark, a blizzard struck. So much snow was falling we couldn't see the road. Then a truck passed us and forced us off the road and the snow covered us up. So there we were. There were four of us in the car—Mother, my sister Peggy, and cousin Don Park. We sat there for hours and hours. We decided we were done for, but knew better than to try to leave the car. All we had to eat was chocolate-covered cherries. Those got us through the night.

Meanwhile, Dad got one of our neighbors and they started walking the highway out of White Deer. We were ten miles out so they were frozen stiff by the time they found us. They pulled us out with a pickup that had chains on the tires. I thought I would never eat another chocolate-covered cherry.

I got my education and taught school awhile, then in 1966 I left Texas to become the superintendent of an international school run by the U.S. State Department in Cairo, Egypt. I taught my sons to ride horses in the shadows of the pyramids. From Cairo I moved back to Texas to Houston, then to Addis Ababa, Ethiopia. Then I moved to Munich, then to Colorado in the United States, to Mexico City, then, finally, back to Texas. And of course I was traveling every chance I got, all over Europe, all around the Mediterranean. I felt at home in all those different places. I always enjoyed adjusting to the different cultures, and I always loved the people. When someone asked me where I was from, I said Texas. Everyone knew where Texas was.

I met a lot of interesting people. John Updike, the writer, visited my schools in Cairo and Ethiopia as part of a State Department program. The most interesting person I got to know was Thor Heyerdahl. While I was in Cairo, he was at Giza building his famous boats out of papyrus. This would have been about 1966 or 1967. Heyerdahl found some guys who lived on Lake Chad, who knew how to work with papyrus, and he asked them to come to Giza to help build the boats. They could only speak their native dialect and French, so he talked to them in French. He flew in planeloads of papyrus and had it all waiting for them. But when they got there they said, "Where's the water?" They told him you have to soak the papyrus in order to work with it, and he didn't know that. So he got the right guys. They knew what they were doing. I went out every weekend to watch them. I asked Heyerdahl to come talk to my school kids, and he said it would make more sense if I bused them out to him so they could see the boat. So that's what I did, and it was great.

—FLOYD TRAVIS, *BUDA,* 1934–99

A Story to Tell for Generations

A young gentleman and young lady met with an experience one night recently, which will be long remembered. They were returning from Terrell to Rockwall when night and a big rain came upon them. They attempted to cross a big ravine that had become swollen. The horses and buggy were washed off the bridge into the foaming water. For a time they were on the brink of eternity. In some miraculous manner they succeeded in cutting the plunging horses loose from the sinking buggy, and by swinging to the harness reached shore with the horses. Stripping the horses of harness, they mounted the animals barebacked and rode to Rockwall, reaching there at 1 o'clock in the morning. The young lady lost her traveling satchel and two hats. The buggy was fished out of the creek the next day and brought to town.

—Source: *Scurry County News,* July 11, 1895

Daughters Are Special

When General William Tecumseh Sherman, commanding general of the United States Army, inspected Texas forts along a new railroad in March of 1882, he brought with him his daughter Lizzie and Winifred Poe, daughter of his aide, Colonel Poe. The girls had quite an adventure. Winifred got to pull the throttle of the train that inaugurated the international railroad bridge over the Rio Grande into Mexico. Two other girls, presumably local, were invited to participate: a Miss Teal, who blew the whistle, and a Miss Hughett, who rang the bell. The engine was decorated with the yellow, green, white, and red of Mexico, while the passenger car wore the Stars and Stripes. Crowds of people covered both banks of the river, and a Mexican military band played "Behold the Conquering Hero Comes" and "Hail, Columbia."

My Dad

My dad, Neal Gentry, felt personally responsible for my daughter Ashley knowing everything she could about nature and the out-of-doors as early as possible in her life. The rest of us were content with the baby talk she was babbling, but Dad took her outside to teach her the names of trees, plants, animals, fruits, and vegetables. He also took the time to teach her to fish. They dug worms, discussed and felt the texture of the soil, and then headed to the lake. Ashley quickly learned about perch, bass, brim, catfish, carp, and gar. Dad's next classroom was a garden full of fruits and vegetables. Soon Ashley was proficient at canning and making jelly or jam. She learned all this long before she started school. My dad's idea is, in addition to a formal education, you have to know, understand, and appreciate all that's around you to be really happy and successful. He's instilled this same knowledge in my brother and me. Dad is eighty-six now and still teaching us about the many blessings that surround us. He thinks eighty-six sounds old, so he has reversed his age and tells everyone he's sixty-eight!

—KATHY ALLEN, OMAHA, TEXAS

While attending Transylvania University in Lexington, Kentucky, **Stephen F. Austin** was enamored with a young lady named Eliza Parker. Eliza married one of Stephen's friends—Robert Todd—and they had a daughter named Mary who married Abraham Lincoln.

Texas's connection with Transylvania U. doesn't end there. One of the university's presidents, Martin Ruter (1785–1838), became the "Father of Texas Methodism."

Folklore Tells Us . . .

- If a bride hears a cat sneeze the day before her wedding, her married life will be happy. I don't know what the result will be if she hears it the day of her wedding, but I'll bet if it's the day after, it's bad news.
- When you see a buzzard, count how many times he flaps his wings until he is out of sight. If he flaps them a lot, your sweetheart loves you a lot; but if he doesn't flap them, she doesn't love you. If you can't find a buzzard, just assume that, wherever he is, he's flapping at least once a second.
- If you have a spider on your wedding dress, you will have good luck. I don't know whether you have to be wearing the dress.
- Nine live red ants worn in a bag around the neck will help a baby during teething. I'll *bet*!

The all-male Texas Legislature voted women the right to vote in state primaries at a special session in 1918.

After he came to Texas, **Sam Houston courted** a nice young lady from Nacogdoches named Anna Raguet. He was twenty-six years older than she was, but that didn't seem to be the problem. Anna wasn't really too sure that he'd

ever gotten a divorce from his first wife. Finally, Sam married the real love of his life, Margaret Lea, of Alabama. Anna died in 1883 at age sixty-four.

Clyde Barrow and Bonnie Parker, the outlaws, were both buried in Dallas, but not together. He's in Western Heights Cemetery, and she's in Crown Hill.

The Colonel and the Girl

Ranald Slidell Mackenzie, first in his class of 1862 in the U.S. Military Academy at West Point, gained the brevet rank of brigadier general during the Civil War. After the war he became the U.S. Army's youngest full colonel, and was assigned to Texas, first to Brownsville and then Fort McKavett. He then took over as colonel of the elite Fourth Cavalry, becoming the most successful Indian fighter in the army, and more than any other, responsible for bringing peace to the frontier. He probably suffered from what today we call post-traumatic stress syndrome because of injuries received in the Civil War.

Mackenzie met Florida Tunstall when she was a beauty about sixteen years old. He couldn't marry, he felt, until he retired from active duty. It wouldn't be fair, with the army moving him all over a vast uncivilized territory. Florida married an army doctor, Redford Sharpe, and lived on several army posts, some at the same time as Mackenzie. Mackenzie suffered hardship and injury, once receiving an arrow during a battle. While commandant at Fort Sill, he fell out of a wagon on his head and was knocked unconscious.

Through it all he was the ultimate professional soldier—aggressive, intelligent, and duty bound. After a brilliant career, Mackenzie, now Commander of the Department of Texas, began to prepare for retirement. Florida was now a widow with a young son who adored Mackenzie. Mackenzie asked her to marry him. She accepted. One night he left her house in San Antonio, and while on a walk, suffered a complete breakdown. The army hustled him off to Bloomingdale Sanitarium in New York. After a hearing he was honorably dis-

charged and remanded to the care of his sister Harriet. He never saw Florida again, and died at the age of forty-nine. Florida lived to the age of ninety-seven, when, in an interview about the frontier days, she did not mention Mackenzie.

On the average, 1,002 men and women get married each day in Texas. That's 501 couples. And there are 915 live births on the average day.

Stephen F. Austin was enamored of his cousin Mary Austin Holley, a beautiful and cultivated widow who visited Stephen while he was trying to bring civilization to Texas. Unfortunately, just as their relationship was getting cozy, he had to hurry off to Mexico on his mule to put out a political fire. He saw her once more, when he was in Lexington, Kentucky, on a trip to raise funds for Texas. Mary Austin Holley was nine years older than Stephen and outlived him by ten.

Air and Space in Texas

The Kiowa-Apaches, who used to hunt buffalo around the Canadian River in the Panhandle, knew how the sun got up there. It was Coyote who did it. He got fed up with having to walk around in the dark, so he stole Fire and Daylight from some guys who were having a dance in a cave. He stole these treasures by putting his tail in the fire and *high-tailing* it out the door. Coyote made Sun and threw him into the sky and told him to go all around and come back so everyone would have his benefits.

Up! Up!

In any great enterprise, there were pioneers who developed the concepts, took the risks, and showed how it's done. Others, often thousands, follow. Here are four Texans who helped get the world off the ground:

★ ★

- Jacob Friedrich Brodbeck, early inventor, 1821–1910
- Samuel Franklin Cody, Father of British Aviation, 1861–1913
- Katherine Stinson, World's Greatest Woman Pilot, 1891–1977
- Wiley Hardeman Post, pioneer in space flight, 1898–1935

Jacob Brodbeck

You'll notice that the four individuals listed above have a common characteristic: they were flighty from time to time. The first, Jacob Brodbeck, who was born in southwest Germany (in the present state of Baden-Württemberg), moved to the German community of Fredericksburg in the Texas Hill Country in 1846. Jacob was an intelligent and upstanding fellow, so people in Fredericksburg gave him plenty to do. He taught school, served as a county commissioner, surveyor, and school supervisor, and **he married Maria Behrens, with whom he had twelve children.** I suppose that about this time, although no evidence survives to substantiate my theory, Jacob must have felt confined, put upon, earthbound, and trapped. He started fiddling with an idea of how to escape—he would build a machine to propel him to parts unknown. First, Jacob built a model of his machine and powered it with a coiled spring. He could wind it up, let it loose, and it would fly. He took it around to county fairs and amazed people; then he built one big enough to ride in. He set up his airship in a field near Luckenbach, where one hundred and thirty-one years later Willie Nelson, the Texas singer-songwriter, would hold his Fourth of July Picnic. But Jacob didn't know this. If he had, he probably would have invented a radio with a future-playback mode to take along. As it was, Jacob wound the giant spring, packed a barometer and a compass on board, attached a boat propeller in case he came down in a lake, climbed into the right comfortable cabin he had built for himself, and turned the spring loose. Jacob, of course, hadn't figured out how to make the spring sustain its energy. The thing leapt into the air, flew across the field and crashed, all in an eye blink.

Samuel Franklin Cody

Meanwhile, in Birdville, Texas, 250 miles northwest of Luckenbach, the **Father of British Aviation** was four years old. I'm going to spend some time on Sam *before* he became an aeronautical genius, since this is the most amazing part of his story, how he got from here to there. We don't know what Samuel Franklin Cody's childhood was like. If he was as hyperenergetic then as later, he must have been a blur. History picks him up in 1874 when an Indian attack, he thought, left him an orphan. (He wasn't, but that's not part of our story.) Sam went to work as a horse wrangler on a ranch in Palo Pinto County, where a Chinese cook taught him how to make kites. By the time he was twenty, he was a trail boss, driving herds of cattle from Texas to Montana. About this time, 1881, he delivered fifty horses to a buyer in England, who turned out to have a daughter named Lela whom Sam promptly married. Now we'll push the fast-forward button, so watch closely. Sam brings Lela to Texas, then sends her back to England for safekeeping when he runs out of money. He travels to Alaska where he prospects for gold for a couple of years, then returns to driving cattle in Texas. In 1887 he joins a Wild West show and performs tricks as Captain Cody, King of the Cowboys. Lela's still in the picture, still loves Sam, and in 1889 gets an excellent idea: Sam should form his own show patterned after Buffalo Bill's Wild West Show. (By the way, Buffalo Bill's middle name was also Frederick: William Frederick Cody. But B. Bill was born fifteen years before our Sam, so they couldn't have been twins.) Lela and two of their sons joined Sam, and they became the toasts of Europe as the Great Codys. They programmed all the usual Wild West attractions in addition to melodramas Sam wrote based on his experiences in Texas and Alaska. They were pretty exotic then, with titles such as *Calamity Jane* and *Klondyke Nugget.*

Europe went crazy over the Great Codys, but show business, with all that adulation, grew dull. Sam started thinking. People were inventing things. The telephone was widespread now, even in wide-open spaces in Texas where he used to drive cattle. He remembered the kite-building Chinese cook those many

years ago. There ought to be something you could do with a kite. Sam always set his goals high, so he built a kite that set a world record of 14,000 feet. The ball of string is an engineering story that we will leave aside. While he's fiddling with this kite, he does some really scientific experiments and gets inducted into the Royal Meteorological Society.

When Sam built a kite that would carry a man to 1,000 feet in high winds, the British army thought, Hey. So our Sam built a few for them, and made a little extra change training the troops to operate them. From things with strings attached, Sam jumped to the concept of the gas-filled, rigid-framed airship, which a fellow named Zeppelin had already built, but not in England. Sam helped the British build their first dirigible. In 1908 Sam moved on to heavier-than-air machines. He was his own research and development department. He built an airplane out of wood, wire, fabric, and a little metal, stuck a gasoline engine on it, and took off on the first sustained powered flight in England. That was so much fun that Sam built other kinds of planes: one that could land on water, one with double wings. He called his biplane Cody's Flying Cathedral, and it was the biggest plane anywhere. He set all sorts of records in his various creations before his Cathedral VI broke up in the air and killed him. He was famous by then, and thousands upon thousands came to pay their respects. As a result of his work, Britain established the Royal Flying Corps.

Katherine Stinson

Back in 1891 while Samuel Frederick Cody was doing his Wild West thing, **Katherine Stinson, the world's greatest woman pilot** was born (not in

Texas, but she got here as quickly as she noticed she wasn't in Texas). She learned to fly so she could teach lessons to earn money to go to Europe to study music. Her zeal for flying soon flew past her musical intentions, and Katherine became the fourth woman to receive a pilot's license. After barnstorming for fairs as the "Flying Schoolgirl," Katherine moved to San Antonio where, in 1913 with her mother and brother, she started the Stinson School of Flying. In the next four years, Katherine Stinson built her own plane, became the first woman to execute the loop-the-loop maneuver, the first pilot to fly at night, and the first pilot to do skywriting at night. She accomplished all this before Amelia Earhart graduated from high school. In 1916 Katherine flew her plane in Japan, impressing the Japanese so much that they formed clubs all over Japan in her honor. She made more than thirty demonstration flights in China. Back in the U.S., she was the first woman to receive a commission as a mail pilot. Then—I'll bet you're tired, but Katherine wasn't—she set a long-distance record flying solo from Los Angeles to San Francisco.

Then Katherine quit flying. Not just like that, and she didn't plan it that way, but World War I intervened. She tried to sign up as a pilot in the military, but they wouldn't let her do that. So she volunteered to drive ambulances. When she returned from Europe after the war, her health wasn't so good, so she moved to Santa Fe, New Mexico, became an architect, married a pilot who became a judge, and lived until 1977—well into the space age.

Wiley Post

And of course there are those Texans who can't stand it if they're not doing something really out of sight. For example, **one Wiley Hardeman Post, our greatest early aviator,** tried to break the law of gravity way before he should have been trying to fool with Mother Nature. Wiley was born near Grand Saline in Van Zandt County in 1898, and saw his first airplane when he was fifteen. He started jumping out of planes with a parachute to entertain the crowds at county fairs, and soon became a pilot. He went to work in the Oklahoma oil fields to make money to buy a plane, but lost an eye in an accident. Wiley's philosophy was not that he lost one eye, but that he had one left. He bought a plane with his workman's comp and kept flying.

While he was barnstorming in Sweetwater, Texas, he fell in love with a young lady named Mae Laine, so she flew with him to Oklahoma to get married. In 1931 Wiley became famous for flying around the world with navigator Harold Gatty, and then in 1933 he became the first person to fly around the world alone. Wiley then decided he was ready to take aviation to a higher level—beyond the atmosphere. So, with the help of engineers from B.F. Goodrich company, he invented the pressurized suit, added a supercharger to his *Winnie Mae*, and took aim at 50,000 feet, discovering the jet streams in the process.

Wiley died young in a crash with Will Rogers, but thirty-four years later, Neil Armstrong walked on the moon in a descendant of Wiley's suit. I'm sure Wiley was tickled when Armstrong announced to the Manned Spacecraft Center in Houston in 1969, "The Eagle has landed."

Wiley's wife, Mae, sold his plane to the Smithsonian. When I was a teenager, I met Mae where she worked, at Drake Hardware near the Lubbock County courthouse. She passed away in 1984.

Moon in Eclipse

People who had occasion to be out to scan the skies Wednesday night were rewarded with a clear view of an eclipse of the moon. The eclipse was visible all over Texas and the night was clear, the moon was exactly full just at the time. The eclipse started at 8:42 P.M. and the shadow passed off at 11:44. About nine-tenths of the moon was covered.

—Source: *The Snyder Signal,* March 13, 1914

Fire in the Sky

I noticed the fireball as it was coming up out of the horizon. It streaked toward me, leaving a full trail of orange fire behind it. It came from west-northwest and passed overhead, going for Florida, all the time silent. I couldn't see the shuttle at the front of the streak. It was as if the fire began there of its own accord. I've watched meteor showers and comets, and this was of a completely different order. The fire did not fade behind the shuttle. It remained in the sky, this wide brilliant stripe from horizon to horizon. I stayed outside until the fire dissipated. And then the sky was pitch black again.

—LARRY SWAYZE, *AUSTIN*

The Lyndon B. Johnson Space Center

As headquarters for American astronauts, the Johnson Space Center—**first called the Manned Spacecraft Center**—in Clear Lake, south of Houston, has become one of the nation's premier attractions. Here visitors from around the world get in touch with the efforts that have made Texas a focal point of space exploration. The Johnson Space Center is one part of a national science-engineering enterprise that includes launch facilities at Cape Canaveral, Florida; a rocket assembly plant in Mississippi; and the Marshall Space Flight Center in Huntsville, Alabama. The facility assumed responsibility as Mission Control in 1964 with the launch of *Gemini 4*, and has carried out its part in innumerable space-related missions since then, including the *Apollo 11* flight in 1969 that first placed Neil Armstrong and Buzz Aldrin on the moon, followed by *Apollo 12*, which included native Texan Alan Bean. These latter-day marvels incorporate the skills of thousands of workers from all different fields and talents, fused in a way that would amaze the pioneers of flight, especially Jacob Brodbeck with his wind-up, spring-loaded airship. The moon, Jacob, the moon!

Commerce-born U.S. Army General Claire Chennault, famous for heading up the Flying Tigers of World War II, was related to Sam Houston on his father's side and to Robert E. Lee on his mother's. To stretch a little farther, the originator of the phrase "the eyes of Texas are upon you," William Prather, was pall bearer at the funeral of Robert E. Lee.

Texas Cuisine

If you like terrific food and you're in Texas, you're in the right place. The rich cultural mix of our past and present has produced an alarming variety of delicacies. You'll find Southern style, Mexican, Cajun, Chinese, Vietnamese, German, Czech, and cowboy. All over the state, farmers produce tomatoes, green beans, black-eyed peas, corn, okra, yellow squash, onions, and zucchini, and during the summer months you're likely to be served all these on any home table. Local folks can, or "put up," these good things in Mason (or Kerr) jars to consume over the winter, and they are treasures when presented as gifts with a bow of ribbon tied around the lid.

Being Texans, **we eat a fair amount of beef,** which one old-timer assures me, "there's nothin' healthier than." The red meat controversy hasn't made many inroads among folks whose grandparents lived to a hundred eating beef one to three times a day. Of course those same folks, most of them, had fresh garden produce to go with their helpings of animal protein. And they got all that exercise chasing around after oil gushers and maverick cattle, so there you go.

Charlotte's No-Recipe Chicken-Fried Steak

Author's Note: I have tried chicken-fried steak all over the country, and there is a lot of good chicken-fried steak. It has to be, because Texans know the difference. Chicken-fried steak has even had a bit part in a movie. I suppose everyone has seen The Last Picture Show, *from the 1966 novel created by our champion writer, Larry McMurtry. It takes place in Anarene, the nom de plume of Archer City. In the movie, Ben Johnson's character, Sam the Lion, strolls into the café and says "Chicken-fry me a steak." And there it was: a Texas chicken-fried steak, laid right out on the world stage. This was also the momentous occasion when "chicken-fry" became a verb. Well, I don't know how good Ben's chicken-fried steak was, but I know he would have liked Charlotte's.*

I grew up on a farm near Muleshoe. My daddy raised cotton. It was my job to do the cooking. My sister was responsible for doing the dishes, and my two brothers had their chores on the farm. In the fall we all picked cotton twice a day, in the morning and evening while it was cool. My mother taught me how to cook chicken-fried steak. She learned to make it by watching my dad's mother, Lula Hamilton Morgan. Lula, who was from around the Goldthwaite area, became the main cook at the Ballinger Hotel in Ballinger. She had ten kids, so she had to know how to cook.

When we raised our own beef, we used home-grown round steak. We tenderized it with a Nehi bottle. We held the bottle upside down and pounded both sides of the steak with the little end of the bottle. You really have to work it over with the bottle before it's tender enough. Mother uses that bottle for her rolling pin now. Usually when I'm rushed for time these days, I buy the steak already tenderized from the supermarket.

You dip the steak three times. First in flour seasoned with onion powder, garlic powder, and pepper. Then I dip the steak in egg and milk. Third, I dip it back in the seasoned flour. While this is going on, you want your grease to be heating. The best frying pan to use is a cast-iron one, but nowadays I use an electric skillet. You don't want your meat swimming in grease. You don't want to deep fry it. You want about a half inch around your meat while it's cooking. Old-fashioned lard is fine, or vegetable oil is fine. You want the grease really hot. Put your steak in and sear it on both sides really quickly, then turn the fire down and let it cook slowly, with a lid on the skillet, so it'll be tender. Turn the meat over several times while it's cooking.

Now you have to practice making chicken-fried steak. You have to experiment with how much seasoning to put in your flour. I mix the proportions by pinch and put, so I don't know how much garlic salt and onion salt and pepper to tell you to put in. But the mix is really simple. You have to develop an eye for when to turn your steak, and when to take it out. That's the best part of the recipe. Practice.

—CHARLOTTE SHULTZ, *AUSTIN*

Chicken-fried steak is one word. It looks like three but it's not. The chicken-fried steak is never referred to as *a steak*. It is understood to be a different entity than red meat, although that's how it starts out. Everyone in Texas considers themselves to be the final judge of the quality of a chicken-fried steak.

Pure Beef Burgers and Fine Chocolate Shakes

My quintessential Texas hamburger joint is located on the main drag in Hamilton. It's called the Dairy Twin, and the name shares the sign with the motto "Pure Beef Burgers." I stopped in to let my senses realign after visiting Davy Crockett's widow's grave in Acton. It was about eight o'clock on a Friday night, and the Dairy Twin was, well, not packed, but busy. The women behind the counter hustled around a compact but complicated kitchen that looked as if its owners had made some adjustment here or there every day for about six months until it just suited them. There was no waste of motion. I liked the décor too. Twenty framed jigsaw puzzles adorned the chipboard walls, pictures of pretty mountain scenes and of a lion and a tiger. A fiftyish man whose luck had run out sixty years ago was trying to order some kind of burger when the proprietor ran out of patience, scribbled something on the green-and-white ticket, and without looking reached behind her and snapped it into a clip over the grill. Then her no-nonsense eyes settled on me. *If you don't pick quick, I'll order for you too, mister.* I had been too interested in the jigsaw puzzles to think about what I wanted, so I scanned the menu and ordered what I read first and second: a Texas Sourdough Burger and a large chocolate shake.

While awaiting my order I noticed the cooks were too busy hustling burgers and shakes and Cokes out to the customers to ask if everything was all right. It seemed they didn't need to. *They prepared it.* So I watched the clientele at the Dairy Twin for any indication of dissatisfaction. Nope. When their trays arrived, they looked upon the offerings with a second's reverence before digging in. So I was feeling pretty optimistic by the time my order arrived.

To start with, the beef was the real thing, just like the sign said, and the sourdough bread was fresh. I had peered into the kitchen to see a lady sitting in a folding chair holding a serving tray in her lap chopping lettuce, so I wasn't expecting an undamaged leaf of lettuce. And I have to admit, this type of lettuce simplifies the construction of the layers, acting like a leveler. You're soon set to take a bite. This one was, bottom line, mighty fine.

Then I was ready to try my shake.

The very best chocolate shakes are those I make myself out of Promised Land All Jersey Whole Chocolate Milk (from Floresville) and Blue Bell Home-made Vanilla Ice Cream (from Brenham). Somebody has usually cheated on bought shakes. The main problem is that it hasn't dawned on the management that the only reason any human being would want to drink one is for the shear, luscious pleasure of it.

So, with trepidation, I tried my first Dairy Twin chocolate shake. It was fine, like those we enjoyed at Mrs. Starr's Drive-In in Sweetwater in the fifties. Consistent from top to bottom. My plastic spoon stuck up in it without moving. It was impossible to drink through a straw. It had passed my first two tests. Now, the taste test. Good. Real ice cream, real milk. Stirred well but not beaten to death.

How to Cook Biscuits in a Dutch Oven

A real outdoors cook places a high value on a good Dutch oven. A Dutch oven is made out of cast iron. It has iron legs about an inch or two long. Some have a skillet handle. The lid has a rim to hold coals. This kind of lid is what makes the whole shebang an oven instead of a frying pan. When you get a new Dutch oven, you have to season it to give it a nonstick surface. You do this by coating it all over with vegetable oil and baking it at about 350 degrees until the oil turns solid. This process creates a coating that would protect the space shuttle on re-entry as well as those tiles NASA uses, but they didn't ask me.

We won't go into the recipe for biscuit dough right now. You can use canned biscuits just fine. First, you build a fire on the ground about an hour before you want to start your biscuits. Any kind of natural wood without coatings will do. The best is some kind of hardwood that will make good coals, like oak or mesquite. Use plenty of wood because you are going to need coals for both the top and bottom. Set your Dutch oven out away from the fire while you put your biscuits in it. You want a little cooking oil on them.

Now, you are going to cook the top of the biscuits first. This is the great secret of biscuit baking. I learned it from Virgie Scrivner, my wife's maternal grand-mother, who was supposed to be taking it easy after surgery. She had been watching me out the back window of a camping trailer as I dumped out the sec-ond of two batches that were charred on the bottom and uncooked on the top. She couldn't stand it. She eased down the steps, cripped over to my fire, and start-ed giving orders. "Drag that oven off the fire," she said, "then after a little bit put your biscuits in." After I did this, she said, "Now put the lid on and shovel it so it's covered with coals. After a few minutes, check to see if the tops are brown. When they're light brown on the top, drag the oven onto the coals and cook the bottoms of the biscuits."

She hobbled back to her easy chair, sat down, and watched to see if I did it right. When the biscuits were perfectly done, I brought them in on a plate for her inspection. "How many biscuits you reckon you would have gone through before you figured that out?" she said, buttering herself the first one.

Buffalo chips were used for fuel if there was no wood. And my grandfather told me buffalo chips were used like paper plates, especially when the cook served pancakes. Of course, you didn't want a new one, he said. It needed to

have been through several seasons under the sun before it was suitably dry, light, and smooth. Proper protocol was, you selected an aged chip, turned it over so the flat side was up, scraped it off with your knife, banged it on your knee, and voilá! A real old-time cook might cook the bacon directly on the buffalo chip for extra flavor.

The U.S. Army on the Texas frontier in the 1860s and '70s had more to do than watch for Indians. For instance, it had to assign contracts for hundreds of thousands of pounds of flour, which contractors transported by wagon and rail from as far away as Chihuahua City, Mexico. The quality of the flour and the resulting bread was the subject of much official correspondence. At Fort Davis, **three soldiers baked 560 loaves each day** of the week except Saturday, when they baked twice that number. At Fort Bliss for awhile one Henry Curley, a civilian, baked for the entire post, and received two sacks of flour a month for his pay. Apparently the army decided his wages were too high or the bread not good enough, for they let him go. Soldiers resumed baking their own bread.

Subsistence Grub

Supplies carried in a pioneer's wagon included potatoes, bacon, beans, flour, salt, coffee, and several Dutch ovens. Chuck wagon food, fixed by the cook on a cattle roundup, might include beef brisket, beans, cherry cobbler (after canned cherries came along), and scratch biscuits—and, of course, hard hot coffee in an iron pot on the edge of the campfire, available around the clock.

Elaine's Crock Pickles

This is a recipe for **old-fashioned crock dill pickles** that my dear mother-in-law, Mable Rogers Schlomach, shared with me. Not only is this a good recipe, it holds special memories for me. On Mother's Day of 1980, we went to visit my mother-in-law and father-in-law at their old rock house northeast of Burnet. This house, built in the 1800s, was the homeplace of my father-in-law as he was growing up. It consisted of two rooms with an attic, but it was home for the family of six. Now in their retirement years, it was home for my mother-in-law and father-in-law. When we came to visit that Mother's Day, my mother-in-law was lying on the couch not feeling well. She never complained, so she wouldn't tell us not to come visit, nor would she tell us how badly she felt. The next day she went to the doctor. She was diagnosed with terminal cancer that took her life within five months—and these final months were spent either in the hospital or recuperating at home after the cobalt treatments. During the time she was at home, family members took turns staying with her and my father-in-law to care for both of them. They always enjoyed gardening and that year was no different. Cucumbers were coming in, and everyone always loved her dill pickles made in a crock. Her recipe has been passed down through the generations. My husband remembers his Grandmother Rogers making these pickles in a large crock when he was a young boy.

One weekend, I told my mother-in-law that I would be happy to put the pickles up if she would share her recipe with me. Here it is:

Crock Dill Pickles (1 gallon)

Place dill, garlic cloves, and grape leaves in a gallon crock (or glass jar). Fill with uniform, medium-sized fresh cucumbers. Combine one cup salt, one cup vinegar, and about 2 quarts of water (well water or distilled water); pour over cucumbers. Cover with plastic wrap and fasten with a rubber band. Leave out unrefrigerated for about a week or until the cucumbers are pickled to desired taste. Then, store in the refrigerator.

—ELAINE SCHLOMACH, *AUSTIN*

Del Rio's **Val Verde Winery** survived Prohibition by selling sacramental wine to Catholic churches on contract. A family, however, could make 200 gallons for its own use (a regulation that still exists). Texans liked wine made from wild mustang grapes that they could pick in the countryside, but also made it from peaches, apricots, plums, blackberries, and whatever else would ferment. It took a wooden wine keg and lots of sugar—about ten pounds per five gallons of wine, depending on how sweet they liked it.

Thomas **Munson** from Denison was the world's foremost authority on grapes and a member of the American Academy of Science. He saved the French wine industry. Facing ruin from phylloxera, a kind of plant lice, France welcomed Munson's solution—graft their grape vines onto **wild Texas Mustang** grape stock, which was resistant to the infestation. The French inducted Munson into their Legion of Honor. Here's to Munson. *Clink.*

What a New Yorker Had to Say

During frontier times, restaurant cookin' was markedly marginal. Travelers, especially those who had frequented the finer establishments of the East, had a hard time finding a spot that was up to their standards. Frederick Law Olmsted, who designed New York's Central Park, had this to say about the food at Austin's finest hotel in 1857: *"Never did we see any wholesome food on that table. It was a succession of burnt flesh of swine and bulls, decaying vegetables, and sour and mouldy farinaceous glues, all pervaded with rancid butter. After a few days, we got a private room, and then, buying wheat bread of a German baker, and other provisions of grocers, cooked what was necessary . . ."*

★ ★

Bearing the above restaurant in mind, which would have been located some-where on Congress Avenue here in Austin where I am writing this, I looked up a report about the *Sardine Rouge*, a present-day restaurant in the same vicinity. I noticed right away how the cuisine is *hautier* than it was in 1857. Here are some of the descriptive phrases the writer used:

spinach-topped oysters

additional soul   aromatic vapor

intimate seating
                              truffle-studded quenelle

silky house foie gras on toast
                              palate-cleansing entremet of sorbet

bistro   *white china tureen*

                              crystal clear like a good consommé
mildly seasoned scallops

              Pernod Sabayon   stained glass window

buoyed by a sauce of
                                        treasured fungus

Seafood Napoleon

Pheasant Consommé   **complimentary appetizers**

tall banquettes   prepared tableside
              white napkins
English pea cream sauce
                              Madeira-spiked au jus

squid-ink-tinted ravioli

mahogany-toned au jus

                                        Alsatian Pinot Gris

atmospheric touches
              unexpected panache

I'm sure **Frederick Law Olmsted** would have been pleased. Oh. I've just noticed that Texas has seventy tortilla factories—more than any other state. I don't know where it ranks in the Pheasant Consommé category.

Pumpkins grown in Lamb County are shipped all over the world. With irrigation, hot sun, and sandy loam soil, they attain a perfect orange color and thick wall that makes them just right to carve into jack-o'-lanterns. The growing season is June through September.

You'll find more fine, small, **family-run restaurants** per square mile in the Rio Grande Valley (which is a plain, not a valley) than in any other part of Texas. These serve traditional, wholesome Mexican food made on the spot from fresh ingredients. You might find enchiladas and tacos here, but if you do they will be made according to a unique recipe. You're more likely to be offered a chicken or beef dish prepared the way the owners would make it for a family get together. Caro's in Rio Grande City is what I'm talking about. If you go by Caro's, check out the huge prickly pear across the street.

Tamales, those mysteries wrapped in corn shucks that President Gerald Ford tried to eat *all* of. Learn from the President's embarrassment. Take the shuck off. But hey, how was he supposed to know? You have to study these things.

Hot and Saucy

A lot of Texans like a lot of hot peppers. At least you'd think so judging by the amount of activity that goes on in their name. At the Texas Fiery Foods Show

Shoot-Out, held in Palmer Auditorium in Austin, some of the winning products were named the following: *CaBoom! Gourmet Sauce, Tears of Joy Tequila Lime Hot Sauce, Pain 100%, Krakatoa!, Pain 85%, Peaches and Scream, Hot Paradise,* and *Jimmy O's Texas Tangy Teriyaki Marinade.*

Jump and Eat

Blackened elephant anyone? Located just up the Rio Grande from Langtry at **Bonfire Shelter is the oldest mass bison-kill site** in the New World. Here, Native Americans feasted on elephant, camel, horse, and bison. Anvil-like limestone blocks indicate that this site was used as a butchering station 13,000 years ago. They stampeded herds of bison over the cliffs to their deaths. Then one day the discarded bones, meat, and fat apparently exploded spontaneously and reduced themselves to ash and burned and brittle bone. Bonfire Shelter is both the oldest and the southernmost example of the jump technique of bison hunting and the only site of this type yet recorded on these margins of the Southern Plains. That's interesting, but what I wonder about is how the Native Americans reacted to this sudden explosion. You know. The scene was like this: the tribe's meat market managers were gathered around the table, when one of the new hires asked the boss if he could chew on that choice tenderloin of mastodon. Kaboom! The new hire wakes up in the river, thinking, "Couldn't he have just said, 'No?' "

Did the supposedly cannibalistic Karankawas prefer Englishmen or Spaniards? Actually, Cabeza de Vaca reported that the Karankawas were appalled by the shipwrecked Spaniards who ate one of their fellow Europeans. So just who were the barbarians here?

Be Sure to Reserve
Your Potato in Ponder

In my opinion, this is classic small-town Texas. About thirty-five miles due north of Fort Worth on Highway 156 is the small town of Ponder. About the only thing the town is known for is the super fine Ranchman's Cafe. It has literally had customers from all over the world and is known by most folks who live within a hundred miles of Fort Worth as being a fun place to visit and have a great meal.

One Saturday night, my wife and I and another couple decided we would drive to Ponder for dinner. Needless to say, the place was busy busy busy. When we entered, the lady asked me if I had reservations—told her no we didn't—she said she would put my name on the list and it would be about a thirty-minute wait. I told her that was OK. Well in about ten to fifteen minutes, she told us our table was ready. After looking over the menu, I decided on a medium-sized (16 oz.) T-bone steak.

Finally the waitress got around to taking our orders—we all ordered a steak of some kind or other. When I gave her my order, she asked me if I would like a baked potato with the steak—sounded good, so I said "Yeah, do that too." Then she looked at me and said, "Well, have you reserved a baked potato?" I told her no I hadn't. She said, "You have to have a potato reserved in order to get one here." Never heard of such a thing. Needless to say, I had fries with my steak as did all the others in my group. The next time we go, I'll have to remember to reserve a potato—don't really need to reserve a seat—can always get a seat even if I have to wait for a while, so I'm gonna call and reserve the potato, but not the seat.

This really is a famous place. Has been there as long as I can remember. At the beginning, they didn't even have an indoor rest room—actually had an old toilet out behind the building. If you were there before 5:00 and needed to potty, you could either use the old toilet or go across the street to the Ponder Post Office. The post office had a bathroom in it and let customers use it if they needed to. President Jimmy Carter's mother, Lillian, ate there once, and actually bought the retired toilet and had it shipped to Georgia. That was after they finally got indoor plumbing in the place. If you're ever in that part of the state, it would be worth your time to visit. Oh yeah, if you do go there, be sure and save room for dessert. They have some of the best homemade pie you can find anywhere. And cobbler. They got peach, cherry, apple, and some kinds of berry cobbler.

Also ate at the Dixie Dog Cafe in Perryton a couple of times. They make a mean cheeseburger. A nice lady there mailed me one of their "gimme" hats. I wanted one cause I never heard of a café named that and besides it was a pretty good-looking cap. Told her I wanted to buy one. She said they were out, but if I would leave my address then she would mail me one when they got more. She did—for free.

—BILL NANCE, *CEDAR PARK*

For Elgin sausage and beef brisket, stop at Southside Meat Market in Elgin, right on Highway 290 as you get into Elgin. Following the tradition of meat markets in this part of the country, the Southside folks will wrap your order in brown paper, sell you a soda pop, onions, pickles, and cheese to go with it, and you take it all back to a table. You need to designate a driver at this point.

The Rio Grande Valley produces citrus that's habit forming. The most famous items are the **Texas grapefruits,** the Rio Star and Ruby-Sweet, descendants of the Texas Ruby Red. They're naturally sweet, and are colored deep red on the inside. The Valley farmers produce more than five million boxes of these delightful orbs each year, weather permitting. One of the best combinations in the culinary universe is a big bowl of sectioned Texas red grapefruit and a big plate of assorted Gulf Coast seafood.

Do you like your alligator rare? If so, you need to visit Rosco, a **very rare** white-skinned American alligator on loan to the Texas State Aquarium in Corpus Christi (he's also been a star visitor at the San Antonio Zoo) from the Audubon Institute in New Orleans. He likes fish and chicken—high quality, like you and I find at a restaurant, except raw (**very** rare)—served in a bucket promptly at 1:30 every day. Rosco loves this yummy diet so much that he's added forty-five pounds to his seven-foot frame in a little over a year (when he got here he weighed in at 131 pounds). He lives in a 3,000-square-foot outdoor bayou that holds 5,000 gallons of brackish water. When discovered, Rosco—who has pretty blue eyes—had seventeen white siblings, all products of a genetic mutation called leucism, much more rare than albinism. **Now for the joke:** If Rosco had been one of two, their baby-sitter (no doubt his maternal **grand***maw***,** Ms. Chomps) could have achieved fame as the ***au pair*** of the **Very Rare Pair** from the ***Mare* Lair.** As it is, he's just the **Fairest of the Rare,** and in the spotlight's **glare.** Now John Phillip Sousa would have liked that. Bet you didn't know that John Phillip, who wrote the rousing march *"Fairest of the Fair,"* played it at the

Texas State Fair in 1895. Oh. I'm ignoring Rosco. I forgot to warn you. While you're visiting him, don't *dare* get too close. You don't want to be the Gulp of the Gulf.

Port Aransas, just across the bay from Corpus Christi, is the **Shrimp Capital** of the World.

To my taste, the best watermelons are **Black Diamonds** grown until ripe in the sandy loam of the South Plains, gathered by the pickup load, iced down, sliced into half-moons, and then served out in the yard on a carpet of Bermuda grass in the shade of an elm tree. It's OK if the juice drips off your elbows. You won't find many Black Diamonds in the supermarket. They don't travel well. So actually, most of them don't, well, travel. You need to know a farmer to get a really good Black Diamond.

In the 1940s we drove from our farm in Hale County to a Mrs. Black's house in Cochran County for Sunday dinner. She served a very nice meal on nice table linens. I have always thought it strange that she didn't set the table. Her beautiful sterling silver was stuck upright in a round tin can in the center of the table and you only took out what you needed.

—Source: Doris Durrett, *Abernathy, Texas*

Cabrito—barbecued goat—is the most delectable delicacy in all of West Texas.

Most Beautiful Red Enchiladas

I created this category especially for **Manuela Valenzuela's red enchiladas.** When you get your order, devote a moment to just look at your plate. See if I'm not right. Manuela and her husband, Javier, run Quintana's restaurant in Wickett. This is in the wide open spaces of Ward County, west of Monahans, mind you, so fill your gas tank before you head out there. Directions? Get off Interstate 20 and drive into Wickett. Quintana's is on the left. Don't mind the unfancy exterior. The good stuff's inside. Now, next thing is, have some consideration. Don't take a bus full of your friends and neighbors out there just before lunch and expect Manuela and Javier to keep up with all of you. There's enough room for, oh, about forty-two people to sit down at one time, counting the steel stools at the counter. The Wickett folks need a place to sit, and several of the local route drivers count on eating at a certain time so they can go on and get their jobs done. And once you have a table, don't go bothering Manuela. She's busy. I may be at the next table waiting on my red enchiladas. Oh. Quintana's closes on holidays. And at three P.M. on Mondays, Tuesdays, and Wednesdays. But Thursdays through Saturdays you've got until 8 P.M.

Wonderfullest Sopapillas

Manuela Valenzuela again. Her sopapillas are about the size of a paperback book and so light they float off while you're trying to pour the honey in them. Now, here again, mind your manners. Good sopapillas made from scratch take a little time. Allow about a half hour.

Ah, The Smell of Vinegar Taffy

About the first of December, as a signal that good things were coming, Mother started up her taffy, spreading a sharp, pleasant smell through the house. I would stand on a chair to look into the saucepan and watch the clear liquid boil

down. When it was thick enough to hold a spoon upright, she dropped spoonfuls of it on a sheet of waxed paper. As soon as it cooled enough to touch, we each took a piece and began to stretch it. As we pulled and folded it, it grew whiter and whiter, gathering air bubbles and becoming stiff. This transformation was amazing. (Taffy was more fun than modeling clay, my other favorite activity in the winter time.) After pulling it, we laid the taffy down and waited. By the next morning you could hit it with a spoon and it would shatter into bite-size shards. Naturally, I thought this delectable candy had existed for a thousand years. Recently my sister found the recipe for me. It was in our mother's 1946 *Searchlight Recipe Book*, put out by *The Household Magazine* and published in Topeka, Kansas. Here it is:

Vinegar Taffy

2 cups sugar
1/8 teaspoon cream of tarter
2 Tablespoons butter
1/2 cup vinegar
Few grains salt

Combine all ingredients. Boil to hard ball stage (265–270° F). Cool enough to handle. Pull until white and porous. Cut in 1-inch pieces and let set until brittle.

Of course, as I said above, we didn't cut it into pieces. It was more fun to hit it with a spoon the next morning.

Festival Food

Food and drink available at the **Thirtieth Annual Rockport Art Festival** in 2000 included the following: hot dogs, Italian sausage sandwiches, hand-dipped

corn dogs, barbecue plates and sandwiches, Baskin-Robbins ice cream, beef fajitas, fajita tacos, fresh-squeezed lemonade, funnel cakes with strawberries, gorditos, hamburgers, lemon chills, nachos, sausage on a stick, stuffed baked potatoes, barbecued turkey legs, and kabobs with shrimp, beef, pork, chicken, and turkey. The festival is given by and for the Rockport Art Colony each Fourth of July. Rockport, on the Gulf Coast near Corpus Christi, is rated as one of the **Top One Hundred Small Art Towns in America**.

The Marble Slab Creamery gourmet ice cream store, which started in Houston in 1983, now has ninety-three stores all the way east to Florida and west to California.

How We Have Fun

We Are Festive

Big Tex, the gatekeeper at the Texas State Fair in Dallas, is fifty-two feet tall. He came to the fair in 1952 as a three-year-old. He started life as Santa Claus for a pageant down the road at Kerens, sixty miles south. Tex is as big as Paul Bunyan. His jeans weigh sixty-five pounds and took seventy-two yards of denim to make. He has a white hat; black eyebrows; a Dan Post, Texas-shaped belt buckle; and a red-and-blue shirt trimmed with white cuffs. Big Tex's steel jaw opens to emit an amplified "Howdy folks!" I watched on TV as the workers put his size 70 boots on him and noticed he's not wearing socks (as a matter of fact, he doesn't have feet). I deduced that he must not be wearing other . . . ah . . . understuff either, even under all that new denim. Is that why Big Tex stands really still? This is a really chaffing problem, but I'll bet it bothers him more than it bothers me. The fair is held in early fall.

I've been to garage sales and flea markets all over Texas and the South, and I am here to guarantee you that the beaten-est one of all, the **Grand Champ,** is at Canton.

Montgomery County holds its **Music Jamboree** in Conroe on the third Saturday each month. It's free, open to the public, and features all kinds of

Texas music, including Cajun, country, western, gospel, Spanish, oldies, polka, western swing, and bluegrass. Bring a lawn chair. Jamming begins at 5 P.M. until show time at 6:30. Proceeds from concession stands and the cake auction fund the jamboree, so plan on eating after you get there.

The Annual Texas Rice Festival at Winnie, first of October, features, let's see, I had it somewhere here. Oh. A rice-cooking contest. Bring your fluffing fork.

On the program for the Texas State Forest Festival at Lufkin is chain-saw sculpting, the Southern Hushpuppy Olympics, and the East Texas Cheerleading Competition. All in one festival.

Troy Aikman received the NFL Man of the Year award in 1997 for his participation in charity work. Of course this is in addition to helping win Super Bowls XXVII, XXVIII, and XXX as quarterback of the Dallas Cowboys National Football League team.

There's always a Texas-sized celebration going on at the San Antonio's River Walk (Paseo del Rio). During the holiday season, thousands of lights spread above the river. There's boat caroling, the Fiesta de las Luminarias, the Lone Star River Walk Holiday Art Fair, and the Rivercenter Christmas Pageant. No kidding. This is about the most festive place you will ever be at around Christmas. At any time of the year, San Antonio is apt to honor its heroes, such as the National Basketball Association champion Spurs, with a boat parade down the River Walk. Sometimes more than 350,000 fans show up to cheer.

You might think about plowing on over to the **Antique Tractor and Engine Show** in Rusk County during April, where they put on a tractor pull. Take your calm pills. There's a lot of tension in this one.

A Wolf Hunt, 1921

This was in December and it was cold as thunder. There was a wolf, I had seen signs of him, and I decided between my dogs and my Steeldust mare I could catch him. So I saddled her up and gathered up my dogs on rope and eased over to McKenzie Mountain. I turned the dogs loose and rode up on the shoulder of the mountain, and that's where I stood my Steeldust mare, right on the east point. I had trained her as a roping horse, and she was a running fool. I set there about a half hour listening to them run, and you could hear the change when they jumped that wolf. I watched it come up out of the brush back toward me and it was a long black lobo, and he was a son of a gun on wheels. When he hit an open spot he stretched it out and left my hounds behind like they was standing still. This wolf, he'd been run before. He was going straight as a wall, then struck sudden to the side so they would go on past him. The hounds they picked it up, and there they all went, around the far side of McKenzie, clear around Little McKenzie and into the Fuller place. They must of run close to an hour over in the Fuller brush before they got him turned. I rode down off the mountain then and stood the mare facing into a little open space so she could get up and go. Here they come, I could hear the mesquite rattling. I had my loop shook out and my Steeldust had her head turned and her ears on the brush, and she was bunched up like a spring.

But what jumped out wasn't a wolf, it was an antelope and my Steeldust mare just jumped out there and caught it. So I laid my loop on it and she sat down and the antelope hit the end of the rope at thirty miles an hour. It went thirty feet in the air and came down thirty feet and killed itself dead as a hammer. I went hand over hand down the rope, and I was just spreading the loop when the antelope come to. It tangled me up in the rope and started kicking. That little antelope cut me all up and kicked holes in my clothes, like to have kicked them all off me. It finally got loose and I was laying on the ground and it just looked back at me, switched its tail, and went on. I don't know where the antelope come from, and I never knew where the wolf went. That was the best trick I ever had pulled on me.

—EVERETT SCRIVNER, 1899–1974
SOURCE: AUTHOR'S INTERVIEW

The Heritage Syrup Festival in Henderson celebrates the area's tradition of making ribbon cane syrup. It's also East Texas's first and largest folk art show. During the first event in 1988, a thousand visitors came to watch an antique syrup mill, powered by mules, crush the cane. If you want to make your sweetie sweeter, mosey on over.

Gruene Hall is the oldest living dance hall in Texas. Pronounced "green," it's where George Strait, Lyle Lovett, and Hal Ketchum played early in their careers. Henry Gruene, a son of Ernst and Antoinette Gruene who came from Germany to settle in New Braunfels in 1845, built the hall to accommodate the social life of the farm families in the surrounding area. He also built a cotton gin, mercantile store, and several Victorian houses. Guess what he named the town? Right. It thrived until the boll weevil decimated the cotton crops and the Depression struck. Today Gruene is reborn as a historic village. The old cotton gin is now a restaurant overlooking the Guadalupe River.

Let's Talk Turkey

The folks up at Turkey (which is twenty-seven miles east of Quitaque) put on a Bob Wills celebration every April. They've also restored their 1927 Gem Theatre and are beautifying the park. Turkey has five churches, a grocery store, a Peanut Growers Association, the venerable Hotel Turkey, almost no turkeys, and about 550 solid citizens. One officer from the Hall County Sheriff's Department provides seldom-needed law enforcement. So don't get rowdy when you drop in to honor the creator of those Texas classics *Faded Love* and *San Antonio Rose*.

Farther south, the **Texas Agricultural Experiment Station** in Yoakum estimates that the poultry business in Gonzales and Lavaca Counties comprises seventy million birds. And that's not a paltry figure.

Around the turn of the century, Brady was known as the **Turkey Capital** of the World. There's a picture of a turkey parade through downtown about that time—hundreds if not thousands of 'em, looking pretty calm. Instructions to the townspeople must have included Words Not to Say Aloud, like, Thanksgiving, Pilgrims, dressing, ax, or cranberry sauce. I drive through Brady quite often and haven't seen any foul parades. Must be a thing of the repast.

Back to Entertainment

Marshall's Wonderland of Lights is created from nine million lights. That's not enough to reach the moon, but they would reach from Marshall to, well, any place that's a thousand miles away. The courthouse alone has 200,000 white lights. Seven hundred thousand visitors from all U.S. states and twenty-two foreign countries had come to take a gander the last time anyone counted. The Marshall enlightenment is part of the Holiday Trail of Lights that runs through Shreveport, Bossier City, and Natchitoches, Lousiana.

The Black Gold Festival in Henderson commemorates the central place of petroleum in the area's economic life.

For many years, tourists visiting Aquarena Springs in San Marcos were entertained by **Ralph the Swimming Pig.** Then the Springs changed from a commercial enterprise to one of research. Ralph went on to piggier things.

The Rockport Seafair in October features crab races. *You* make up the joke.

Top Attractions

- The Alamo in San Antonio
- The River Walk in San Antonio

- Six Flags Over Texas amusement park in Arlington
- Prime Outlet Mall in San Marcos
- Lyndon B. Johnson Space Center in Houston
- The State Capitol in Austin
- Fort Worth Stockyards in, let's see . . .
- Padre Island National Seashore
- SeaWorld in San Antonio
- San Antonio Zoo
- Fiesta Texas amusement park in San Antonio
- Moody Gardens in Galveston

Sports teams from the University of Texas at Austin have appeared on television more times—258—than any other team. As of September 11, 1999, they had appeared in 115 national broadcasts.

The most spectacular Texas college mascot is the **Texas Tech Masked Rider.** He or she, resplendent in a red-and-black costume with mask and flowing cape, gallops a fine black horse around the football field at Jones Stadium, to the cheers of 50,000 fans. Add the Goin' Band from Raiderland charging in off the sidelines, and you have a real Texas-style humdinger of a Saturday.

The most honored college mascot is Texas A&M's Reveille, an American collie. When funeral services for Reveille V were held at Kyle Field in College Station on September 11, 1999, thousands of Aggies and their friends attended.

Some familiar university names and their alter egos: The Longhorns at UT Austin, Red Raiders of Texas Tech, Aggies of Texas A&M, Sun Devils of UT El Paso, Horned Frogs of Texas Christian University, the Baylor Bears, and the SMU Mustangs.

In the summer of 1999, **cyclist Lance Armstrong,** who grew up in Plano and lives in Austin, won the 2,400-mile Tour de France. This terrific win came three years after he was diagnosed with advanced testicular cancer. Doctors called it "the greatest medical sports comeback of the twentieth century." While in France, Lance hung a Texas flag on the back of his warmup van.

Roller-coaster boosters boasted about the Texas Giant at Six Flags Over Texas by voting it the top wooden roller coaster in the country.

Flower Time

The bluebonnet became the Texas state flower in 1901. They let us know that spring in Texas is here. They're here when Easter is here. So when they dress up the landscape, we know to don our pastel hues. During April when bluebonnets are at their peak—especially after a wet winter—we like to drive the wildflower trails through the country around towns like Llano, Burnet, or Brady. On Sundays we like to dress our children and grandchildren in their finery and take their pictures on the roadsides among the bluebonnets.

Other wildflowers you're likely to see:
- Texas star, a daisy-like plant with a five-petal, yellow flower.
- Indian paintbrush, similar in shape to bluebonnets, but mostly orange, although my favorites are the lemon yellows on FM 103 between Nocona and Spanish Fort.

- Firewheel, or Indian blanket. Red in the middle and yellow around the edge. In milder climates, they sometimes bloom year round.
- And verbena, pink evening primrose, yellow primrose, horsemint, prickly poppy, and Mexican hats.

More than 5,000 species of flowering plants are native to Texas. Grasses account for 523 of these, according to Frank W. Gould of Texas A&M, who paid close attention to such things.

Are all those spring blankets of red, yellow, white, and blue wildflowers really wild? Well, yes, but they have a little help from our friends at the Texas Department of Transportation, which cares for more than 700,000 acres of road-sides. Staff members groom, fertilize, mow, and plant shrubs and trees. Each fall they help nature out by spreading about 60,000 pounds of wildflower seeds along the roadsides.

Tip from the wildflower experts at TXDoT: for stable, healthy stands of plants, you should combine wildflowers, legumes, and grasses.

March, April, and May are prime wildflower time. Around the end of March and first of April, look for dogwood festivals in Tyler, Woodville, and Palestine. **I** spent a spring week in East Texas where plenty of rain falls, and the pink evening primroses were astonishing, forty and fifty acres of them with fat horses grazing in the middle.

We Are Sporty

The famous frontier marshal Bat Masterson turned boxing promoter for prize-fighters John L. Sullivan and Jim Corbett. He also attended the controversial boxing match between Bob Fitzsimmons and Peter Maher staged by Judge Roy Bean near Langtry, Texas, in 1896. The judge arranged for a ring to be built on a sand bar in the Rio Grande where federal law didn't apply. Photographs show that the promoters built a high, solid fence around the ring so only those fans who paid admission could watch the bout.

On the first weekend of November 1997, the **scores of all winning high school football teams in Texas** totaled 12,573 points, while the losers racked up 3,748. Until you found out just now, I was the only one who knew, because I added them up.

On April 13, 1942, in Augusta, Georgia, **two great Texas golfers** went into an eighteen-hole playoff for the Masters championship. Byron Nelson beat Ben Hogan 69–70.

Texas is a racy state. The Wiener Dog Nationals is held at the Gulf Greyhound Park in Galveston. It's the world's oldest, largest, and no doubt longest, wiener dog racing event. Whether they serve hot dogs, I can't say.

The Corpus Christi Greyhound Race Track is located at 5302 Leopard Street. So you can spot them as they go by. Bark bark.

Favorite Things for a City Slicker to Do at a Dude Ranch:

- campfires on the range
- chuck wagon meals
- country-western dancing
- horseback riding
- listening to ranch dance fiddling
- pitching horseshoes
- sittin' on the corral
- sunrise and sunset excursions
- watching cowboys ride horses and rope and brand cattle
- wildlife photography

The city of Fort Worth reenacts its **historic cattle drives** each day during the summer. Six drovers ride herd on fifteen Longhorn steers so tourists can see how it really was. In true cubicle-age fashion, the steers undergo **rigorous testing** to make sure they can stand the noise of crowds and cars. When you drive this breed through a bunch of tourists, you got to be careful. The ancestors of these steers had to build up a lot of "mean" to survive in the wilds of Texas before the Civil War.

Saved by the (Cow) Bell

During the Civil War a federal detachment energetically surrounded the mansion belonging to John H. Wood, one of the founders of Rockport. However,

they mistook a herd of cows that were milling around the house for Confederates and beat a quick retreat. The only accolade the beef got, however, was a satisfied "well done!" Yuk yuk.

Education and the Arts

Education

One thing you notice pretty quick about this "cowboy country" is that learning centers of an astonishing variety are tucked nearly unnoticed into the landscapes of every town and city, and some far out in the country. There are private schools, and public schools, and theological seminaries, and institutes of technology, and of culinary arts; there are universities and branches of same; there are community colleges and junior colleges, and Montessori schools, and centers for entrepreneurial education. In Texas, you can just pick a subject, and there's a place to learn it, probably within walking distance. And up in the Texas Legislature, when it meets, half of every conversation and three quarters of every proposed bill has something to do with education.

Beginnings

One of the factors generating the Texas Revolution was Mexico's failure to establish a public education system. In these raw new areas, settlers harbored a cultural nervousness about allowing the children to go untutored. In the absence of established schools, farmers, ranchers, and sawmill workers put up their own. Many of today's 1,000-plus local Texas school districts began as a one- to four-room building in the middle of a pasture with five or six students.

The settlers typically named these schools after one of the families whose children attended them, or after the person who owned or donated the land, or after a nearby stream, hill, or other geographic entity. So for many years there was a Frog Holler school located on Frog Hollow near Newport. The schools were located more or less equidistant from the original families.

The parents formed a school board and hired a teacher (often a young female relative scarcely older than some of her prospective students), and proceeded to "Give those children some learning."

Most of the children, both boys and girls, could ride a horse by the time they were five or six, and they got themselves to school, sometimes two to a pony, unless there was a hard storm blowing. Winter was a good time for heavy-duty schoolwork, since parents were less likely to pull their kids out to attend to plowing or picking or branding. If a norther blew in during the middle of the day, the teacher was apt to set her students to stuffing quilts and towels around doors and windows to keep her charges warm and dry until the weather improved. The arrangement known as a one-room school in which all grade levels learned together wasn't as primitive as moderns often assume. For instance, although former students tend to remember mostly the shenanigans that went on, younger students sat next to their elders, who, for better or worse, became role models to follow. Surviving evidence also says that surprisingly many the teachers were good. And it's a pretty sound educational experience for a child to participate in a spelling bee with children of all ages.

Good Kids

Teachers, poorly paid, had to live with families in the community. The teachers usually came to teach when they were young, and many stayed on to teach several generations within the same community. Many married local gentlemen. Generally they were devoted to their students.

One lifelong teacher I know, Verle Latimer, brought to a family reunion in

1996 a little jewelry box from which she drew perfectly preserved school pictures she had saved for sixty years. The dates on them began in the 1930s. Many were taken when people at the reunion—now grand- and great-grandparents—attended her classes in Cotton Center as second and third graders. She passed them around.

Her former students adjusted their trifocals and smiled, looking. One wife nudged her husband of four decades. "Look at that innocent little boy," she said.

"Still am," he said.

The state was slow to make school attendance compulsory—which it did in 1915, and then only required students ages eight to fourteen to attend two months per year. Noting surprisingly little outcry, the legislature soon eased the bar upward. Children between six and sixteen had to go to school a full nine months.

When the **Texas State Library and Archives** opened during the days of the Republic, the Texas Congress appropriated $10,000 to buy books. However, only one—the *Edinburgh Encyclopedia*—was purchased before attention was diverted by strife with Mexico and troubles between settlers and Native Americans. Later, the library did grow, but was **wiped out by fire** when the state capitol building burned. Of course, in true frontier fashion, the new plans were for bigger and better things. Today the main storage facility for historical documents is the pink granite Lorenzo de Zavala State Archives and Library Building east of the State Capitol Building in Austin. The Sam Houston Regional Library and Research Center in Liberty also has a fine collection.

In 1918 **George Washington Littlefield** bought the 5,300-volume John W. Wrenn private library in Chicago for $225,000 and gave it to the University of Texas. The Wrenn collection is strong on the literature and political history of England.

Public Schools

Some facts to figger:

- Texas has more than 7,000 public school campuses, of which about 1,100 are regular high schools.
- The student enrollment is nearly 4 million.
- Fourteen percent are African American, 38 percent are Hispanic, 45 percent are white, and 3 percent are from other ethnic groups.
- Nearly half of all students are considered economically disadvantaged under federal guidelines.
- The attendance rate is about 95 percent.
- The annual dropout rate is under 2 percent, and
- The number of graduates for the class of 1997 was just above 180,000.
- The student-to-teacher ratio is about 15 to 1.

In the fall semester of 1998, more than 530,000 Texans were public school students who were identified as limited English proficient. Of these, approximately 270,000 were served in bilingual programs, 210,000 in English as a second language, and nearly 50,000 in special education.

Texas was one of only a dozen states recognized for the progress it has made toward reaching the **National Education Goals,** which were established ten years ago. The bipartisan National Education Goals Panel commended Texas for its strong improvement in student test scores and for its overall improvement.

Texas was the only state to receive an A for the high quality of its teachers, according to a report issued by the Thomas B. Fordham Foundation. The report says, "Texas earns top honors for its state-of-the-art teacher-quality system."

The enrollment of Texas school districts varies widely, from fewer than 20 at Ramirez Common School District in South Texas, to more than 200,000 in Houston Independent School District. Although the nine largest school districts in the state have at least 50,000 students each and serve 21 percent of all Texas public school students, 34 percent of the districts serve only 2.4 percent of the students. Translation: Texas has a lot of school districts with small enrollments.

In a program called the **Texas School Improvement Initiative** (TSII, which is coordinated by the Texas Education Agency in Austin, monitoring teams made up of practicing school superintendents, principals, and central office personnel visit their peers in other districts. These teams look at areas such as governance (school board and superintendent), the district's planning and decision-making process, and so on. The visiting teams give advice on how to improve situations, and maybe get some ideas to take back to their own districts. As a result of interactive programs such as TSII, Texas's accountability system and student testing programs earn a lot of praise.

Many districts deal successfully with logistical problems that most people would think unsolvable. For example, Mission Independent School District in the Rio Grande Valley has a very high mobility rate among students because many of them are members of migrant families that follow the crops. Yet the students' test scores are high. This district pioneered the use of disaggregated data, which is widely used to see whether particular groups of students need more help.

Although the National Parent-Teacher Association (PTA) was founded in 1897, it wasn't until Oct 19, 1909, that Ella Caruthers Porter, age sixteen, founded the **Texas Congress of Mothers and Parents** in Hillsboro with five members. That was for white parents. African Americans had to start their own organization, the **Texas Congress of Colored Parents.** The two groups did not join until after their national organizations merged in 1970. In 1999, the 90th anniversary of the state organization, the membership was 754,000.

The most popular high school mascots in Texas are:

- Eagles (64)
- Bulldogs (56)
- Wildcats (47)
- Tigers (42)
- Panthers (39)
- Mustangs (32)
- Hornets (27)
- Cougars (25)
- Lions (23)
- Indians (22)

Some of the more unusual school mascots include:

- Grandview Zebras
- Itasca Wampus Cats
- Springtown Porcupines
- Progreso Red Ants
- Hamlin Pied Pipers
- Knippa Rockcrushers
- Hutto Hippos
- Killeen Kangaroos
- Port Lavaca Sandcrabs
- Robstown Cottonpickers

—Sources: Carole Keeton Rylander, Texas Comptroller of Public Accounts (www.window.state.tx.us); Dent Gilley's Texas High School Mascots Page; and, as usual, Bill Nance.

The Itasca Wampus Cats's Football Season, 1964

Coaching in small-town Texas can be one of the most heartwarming and rewarding professions one can hope to have unless the hometown youngsters go zero and ten. When that happens, life is almost to the point of becoming suicidal.

During the football season of 1964, it was my pleasure to work as assistant coach with the greatest bunch of kids that anyone could hope for. They responded to the coach's every direction, worked hard, were good students, trained religiously, and played the game with all their heart and soul; however, needless to say, they just weren't good football players. Small and slow—couldn't block or tackle—couldn't kick, throw, or catch the ball, but they all had hearts as big as a bucket.

During the '63 season, the Wampus Cats finished second in the district with an 8–2 record. The district championship was claimed by the Clifton Cubs on a brisk fall evening in November in one of the best-played football games I witnessed during my thirteen-year coaching career. The fans in Itasca talk about that game to this very day. We had fifteen seniors on that particular team, and all had a wealth of talent.

The '64 edition of Wampus Cats football was far different from the previous year. Due to the absence of a group of seasoned seniors, the situation appeared hopeless from the very beginning.

The head coach of the previous season had moved on to Whitesboro and a new, young head coach was employed to lead the team to victory. All of the fans knew that '64 would be a rebuilding year, but they didn't realize that could mean not winning even one game.

At the beginning of the season, all the fans were reasonably supportive. They knew we had a tough schedule, and we had been picked to finish last in the district. Even with that instilled knowledge, they still thought we should win at least half of our games. Friday night after Friday night the outcome was the same—Itasca loses another game. The kids gave their all—even played real close in some of the games, but the fans wanted another winner. Needless to say, they took their frustrations out on the coaches. If a kid dropped the ball, it was the coach's fault. A missed block was the coach's fault. Missed tackles also became the coach's fault. Little did the fans know how difficult it is to convince a group of young men to go back out there on the field week after week to perform for their parents and other fans. When you ain't winning, the coach has to look for small victories to keep the kids going. The coach has to remember the good block or good tackle made during a game the team lost by a 52–0 score. That's kinda hard to do sometimes.

It was interesting to see how the hometown "good ole boys" treated the coaches away from the school during the 0–10 season. Folks wouldn't even speak to you in the post office or anywhere else in town. Some would cross the street to the other side if they saw you coming up the sidewalk. We sometimes visited the local drug store to drink a malt or eat some ice cream. The entire place would empty within minutes after we arrived. The only friend we had was each other, and there were only two of us. This abuse didn't stop when the season ended either. Those good ole boys had excellent memories. They played every game over and over all winter long. They *won* every one of them too.

Well, fate gave us some relief during the early spring of '65. The local bank allegedly had some shady dealing with one of the good ole boys, and the bank examiners discovered the goings on. They sent in the FBI for a full investigation. The bank was closed for several days, and it appeared it was going to close permanently. People in that town were upset—bad upset. Now they had something else to talk about other than the '64 football season. I remember that the other coach and I rode around and around that bank until the wee hours of the morning the first day the FBI appeared. We couldn't help but feel relieved that this Act of God had delivered us from our misery.

The really sad thing about all of the above is that the parents and fans didn't have a clue as to what a great bunch of kids we had or how hard they worked. They put everything they had into every game they played but were never good enough to win even one game. I left Itasca at the end of the 1964–65 school year to take a head coaching job of my own. The head coach I left behind took that same group of kids and won five games with them during the '65 season. He was also the girls' basketball coach and took that team to the regional finals both years he coached them. All of his work and the work of the kids went unnoticed during 1965–66 'cause they fired him anyway at the end of the year. All because of the 0–10 record of 1964. They would have fired him at the beginning of the season in '64 if he hadn't had a two-year contract, and they couldn't afford to pay him off.

The head coach and I continue to be the closest of friends. We still sit and talk about our coaching days at Itasca and how much we enjoyed working with the kids there. We can even laugh about the '64 season and all we encountered during that miserable year.

I guess the one thing we really learned during that time is *if you're gonna coach football in small town, Texas, you'd better win 'um all or at least most of them* or you can call the U-Haul company come spring.

During the 1965–66 school year, I was the head football coach at Sanger, my hometown. Had a bunch of big kids, and the fans thought we would win the district. We lost the first four games we played. Finished the season with a 5–5 record. If I hadn't had a two-year contract, the Board of Education would have fired me. The second year, we finished second in a much tougher district with a group of great kids that the fans knew couldn't win—but they did win. I could have run for mayor the second year and won.

Small town Texas football is everywhere. Itasca, Sanger, Granger, Hutto, Shiner, and all the others—they're all the same breed: win or move.

—BILL NANCE, *CEDAR PARK*

Missed Again

Once upon a time there were two colleges, **Henry College in Campbell and East Texas Normal College in Commerce.** They both needed students.

Henry College, named for its founders, Henry T. Bridges and Henry Easton, opened in 1892. Bridges provided $15,000 to build an administration building. The school got off to a rousing start. The enrollment for the 1896–97 school year was 220. It seemed Bridges and Easton had a good thing going.

But then Mr. Bridges made a mistake. He tried to entice students from East Texas Normal to come to Henry College.

William L. Mayo, head of East Texas Normal, complained publicly that Henry College was advertising for students in East Texas Normal's newspaper. Well! Mr. Bridges thought that Mr. Mayo just ought to keep his mouth shut. Bridges hitched up and rode the eleven miles to Commerce to demand that Mayo publicly apologize. When Mayo refused, Bridges fired two shots at him, missing both times. Then Bridges gave up on the gun, jumped out of his carriage, and began beating on Mayo with his horsewhip, whereupon the police escorted both eminent educators to the local *calaboose*.

Released on bond, Bridges returned home where community members held that role models for their children should not (1) miss twice at point-blank range and (2) involve themselves in such unsettling public displays. They chastised Mr. Bridges, and enrollment at his school dropped.

Mr. Bridges had not finished his trip downhill. In 1897 the administration building at Henry College burned. The school struggled on under decreased enrollment and dwindling funds, until it closed in 1901. A new institution, Emerson College, opened on the same site in 1903.

Back in Commerce, William Mayo's East Texas Normal College became Texas A&M University-Commerce with a 1998 enrollment of 7,600.

Texas Women's University in Denton is the largest university primarily for women in the United States.

Texas colleges and universities enrolled nearly one million students in 1998.

Higher education systems in Texas are:
- Texas A&M University System with 12 colleges and universities
- Texas State University System with 9
- University of Houston System with 4
- University of Texas System with 13

In 1913 Dr. J.M. Kuehne, Adjunct Professor of Physics at the University of Texas, displayed color photographs of the campus. He created the photos by using dyed starch grains, a process called the Lumiere method.

More than 80,000 Texas band students entered the 1999 All-State tryouts.

Texas Sportswriter's Football Stylebook

If you want to be a sportswriter in Texas, you have to know the lingo. For those who might have such aspirations, I've collected a glossary of phrases that will help you a great deal. The sequence of these terms doesn't matter. You just need to use most of them in every Saturday morning's paper.

16-yard gain on the first play

elected to take it to the air

struggled to an 0–3 start

perfect record

overmatched

margin of victory

dropped a 55–12 decision

attacking style defense

rare 2–0 start

clash of unbeaten teams

jaunt to the end zone

sprinted away down the sideline

impressive win

looking strong

blitzing defense

winless and scoreless on the season

mentally fresh

powers past

blown out

great expectations

chance to prove itself

failed to move the ball

post a win

rare loss at home

power sweeps

mixed the run and pass

a 30-yard option keeper

dismal performance

offense awakens

erupts early

no reason to doubt they could win it all

complete the rout

slammed the door shut

tossed

offense caught fire

blowing anyone off the blocks

pursuit angles

season-ending injury

off-balance

banner year

first pass attempt was intercepted

scoring toss

rambled

got beat by a good team

shocking win

compound fracture

routed

really shut us down

great effort

career rushing record

put the game away

starting to pick up momentum

scoring passes

connected

offensively firing on all cylinders

awesome display of running

rallies late

outstanding individual efforts

eliminated

started the season with two victories

The Prince and the Sesquicentennial Cake

Every seventh grader in the Austin area school district has to take a semester of Texas history. As a state, Texas has a bigger-than-life image and a definite stereotype of excessive pride. The textbook for this class was double the size of my U.S. history book, which indicates that perhaps there was a reason for these stereotypes.

I can't say this was a class I enjoyed that much. For some reason the only lecture that stuck with me was "How Barbed Wire Changed the Face of Texas." But as a kid who earned her parents those hated "My child is an honor student" bumper stickers, I studied and did my homework, despite not being terribly interested.

As a result, I was selected as one of the students invited to a very special event. That year was the Texas Sesquicentennial celebration (a word that was on every spelling test for a whole semester). Honor students from junior high schools all over Austin were invited to be served a piece of the largest cake ever made. And to cut the first slice? Prince Charles!

On the day of the ceremony, our Texas history teacher gave us a big talk about what an honor this was, complete with a dress code and code of conduct to follow. We met at the school that night, and boarded hordes of school buses on a trek to the city coliseum. It was unusually quiet for a pack of twelve-year-olds, but we were all dressed in our finest and very unsure of what was ahead.

Filing into the bleacher seats of the stadium, again it was an unusually civilized scene. There was little talking between me and my neighbors, and teachers were having no problem controlling us. Sitting in a facility familiar to me for basketball games, looking down at the floor, there indeed was the biggest cake ever made.

There were people surrounding the cake on all sides, the women who had baked and assembled this gigantic dessert. There were speeches explaining the process, giving the exact weight and dimensions, but we were all just gaping at this monster cake.

Without further ado, Prince Charles appeared from a side door. He did not take the route so many people do when visiting Texas; he did not try to garb himself as a native, in stiff-looking Wranglers, bolo ties, or boots. He sported full-fledged Prince of England attire, a very regal red coat, with epaulettes and gold braid. Whipping out a fussy little saber, he cut a big wedge, wrestled it onto a paper plate, took a big bite, and was off.

After that, we were all herded to the floor to accept our own piece of cake. Walking out the front doors, a huge line had formed as they opened up the celebration to the general public. I remember passing a shirtless guy with a Texas-sized belly and

a huge python around his neck. But the impression had already been made; Prince Charles in his full princely outfit had lent an air of solemnity to the occasion. His presence, as strange and unrelated to the event as it was, had made me think about what a wonderful place this was to grow up.

I saved my piece of cake, being careful of it on the much rowdier bus ride back home. For some reason, I wanted to keep it, so I wrapped it up and kept it in the fridge.

—DANA WHITNEY GARD, *SAN FRANCISCO*

★ ★

Just Amazin'

I couldn't decide whether to put these under Amazing or Best:

- At the Cotton Bowl game in Dallas on January 1, 1946, Bobby Layne of the University of Texas scored all forty points that his team scored. He rushed for three touchdowns, passed for two more, caught a 50-yard bomb, and kicked four extra points. The final score was 40–27, Texas over Missouri.
- Former Texas Ranger (No. 34) Nolan Ryan threw 5,714 career strikeouts.
- Schoolboy Michael Carter from Dallas threw a 12-pound shot 81 feet, 3½ inches. The record has been standing for twenty years.
- "Slingin'" Sammy Baugh's 51.4-yard punting average for 1940 and career punting average of 45.1 yards are still untouched.

Homing pigeons owned by San Antonio newspapers flew the sports news and camera film from Austin to San Antonio from 1919 until about 1950.

Graduation

In Smithville, a town of about 4,000 in Bastrop County forty-two miles southeast of Austin, there was a lot to do to get ready for high school graduation in May 1999. Families had to prepare food and clean house, because extended family and friends were coming. There had to be plenty of places for everyone to sleep. Sometimes visitors were consigned to pallets in the living room. Several tents were set up in backyards. There were more pickup campers and motor homes in town than usual. It was a good opportunity to visit, sitting around the kitchen table.

★ ★

One person who didn't sit around the kitchen table much was the Senior of the house. The Senior had to get ready for the Senior Party, which was going to feature a live band. The Senior was on the way to or from slumber parties and daytime receptions in various other homes. Usually the Senior could only get into a car that already had five or six people in it. Seniors turned up driving four-door family sedans they had never driven before.

These Seniors were participating in one of the greatest rites of passage that can happen in Texas. This occasion signifies that the community, the churches (there are more than twenty in Smithville), and the school have done all they can. Local businesses have contributed to countless fund-raisers for countless good causes; churches have taken these fine young people on innumerable retreats and outings; the school district has sent its teachers to training in distant places so they could better conduct programs in academics, special education, gifted and talented education, bilingual and English as a second language, general music, choir, band, and art; and coaches have taught their charges How to Deal with Both Success and Adversity.

Yet in 1996, Smithville ISD decided its 1,700-plus students could use some more polish, so it launched a character education curriculum during the 1997–98 school year. The district had this to say:

> We believe that our democracy is based on the assumption that the character traits listed below are accepted values, and that all individuals can demonstrate personal and social accountability. The following character traits will be modeled by teachers and integrated into the curriculum across all grade levels and subjects.

Month	Character Trait
September	Honesty
October	Responsibility
November	Compassion

★ ★

December	Perseverance
January	Loyalty
February	Justice
March	Self-Reliance
April	Self-Discipline
May	Integrity

So now (Smithville hopes) all the Seniors are honest, responsible, compassionate, persevering, loyal, just, self-reliant, self-disciplined, and have personal integrity. Just the sort you would lend your new Buick to.

Smithville held its graduation at the football stadium where there are plenty of bleachers. It was a warmish day. The Crawfish Festival was going on, and many parents were on that committee, proceeds of which were going to the recreation center. There was Crawfish Youth bull riding, and scholarships and awards were handed out to high school students. Then there was a 5K run and a golf tournament. One of the highlights, by the time it was all said and done, was a silent auction at which an elaborate dinner cooked and served by the mayor, including a ride in a limousine, was sold for $1,200. The word was, it was worth every penny. There was a horseshoe tournament that many who didn't want to run in the 5K participated in with gusto. Then came the final band concert by kids who had been in band together since sixth grade. They played the Fight Song for the last time, then looked at each other as if wondering what to do next. They got up and milled around, hugging and patting, and there were quite a few tears.

The Band Must Go On

I accepted a job as band director in Junction in the middle of the 1976 school year. The superintendent of the school district called me on a Saturday, interviewed me on Sunday, and offered me the job at the interview. Junction seriously needed a good band director, and I had to be available immediately. The previous spring the band had received a IV in concert and a V in sight reading on a scale of I to V, with V being the lowest rating that can be awarded. Then, in the fall, the director withdrew the band from the Marching Contest and, during the Christmas holidays, resigned his position. As a result of the band's not participating at the Marching Contest, the University Interscholastic League (UIL) committee suspended them from participating in *all* UIL events. This is about the worst thing that can happen to a band. Being disqualified from going to the contest is similar to an athletic team being barred from playing for a conference title—it removes one of the big reasons for a kid (and band director) to show up for practice.

Junction deserved better. The town, whose population usually hovers around 2,500, is located in Kimble County at the confluence of the North Llano and South Llano Rivers right on the edge of Texas Hill Country. Because of the beautiful setting, several resorts are located in the vicinity, and it's a favorite destination for deer hunters and winter Texans. Cattle, sheep, and Angora goats are raised on the ranches. The people work hard, and they set a good example for their kids.

I arrived in Junction to find the band in disarray, of course. There were about eighty students in the high school band (grades 8–12). The kids' and parents' expectations were low, to say the least. They just wanted the Junction band to "be as good as Robert Lee's." Robert Lee is a "neighboring" town about 120 miles northwest of Junction. At my first meeting with the band boosters, they all applauded politely and nodded knowingly when I proclaimed that we would be *better* than Robert Lee. But even though they may have thought I was daft, they stayed with me, supporting me and their children through the process of rebuilding.

Although some of the kids asked me why I would want to teach band in Junction, they were eager to get to work. In fact, they turned out to be some of the greatest kids I've ever worked with. We worked through the spring semester playing concerts for community events and marching in parades, and little by little the kids began to gain a sense of pride in their band. Included in the "things we always do" was a rule that no matter what happened, the show must go on. If we marched in an event such as the Kimble County Horseracing Association parade and had to march behind the horses, we just did it, no questions asked.

The following fall, the University Interscholastic League reinstated the Junction band program. We were free to compete again! Our weekly performances became doubly important, because they were precursors to the fall Marching Contest.

Home-game halftimes were always interesting, because we played them at the local horse-racing track. The grandstand at the finish line served as the home team's stands, and visitors sat in portable bleachers and parked on the infield grass of the dirt track, which was usually dead and brown by October. Rainy days produced a muddy obstacle course from the stands to the field, and long dry spells produced a man-made dust storm when those visitors drove in. But we marched on through the fall, overcoming every obstacle, practicing our motto that, No Matter What Happens, The Band Must Go On.

The greatest test of this newfound determination came at an out-of-town game. That Friday we boarded the buses and made the forty-mile trip to play Mason, one of our toughest football opponents. As visitors, the Junction band marched first. The sky was cloudy, but I was oblivious to any impending bad weather—as were most of the fans at this hotly contested rivalry. Included in my responsibilities was announcing for our band when our regular announcer could not be there. Such was the case that night.

Since the press box was a crow's nest atop the metal-roofed stadium, I had to climb a two-by-four ladder that went about fifty feet straight up. Once I made the climb, I was faced with a wooden walkway that a mountain goat would have trouble traversing. I had just finished the opening announcements when I heard the first sounds of thunder. Fearing for the students' safety, I immediately began the trek back down the ladder. By the time I reached the ground the rain had started, but it hadn't deterred the Junction kids. They just kept on blowin' and goin' right through the show. When they came off the field, the drum major pointed them toward the buses and they took off in a mad dash. All made it without a problem except one French horn player, Jackie Owens, who tripped over the steel cable that fenced the cars off the playing field. His French horn was flattened, with the bell folded over like a clam. He met me at the door of the bus expecting me to explode, and when I saw his horn, I did—with laughter.

The Marching Contest approached. The band kids, from the littlest eighth grader to the most "famous" senior, knew that our rating would let the town know for sure whether the Junction band was back in business. The kids worked harder than I've ever seen a bunch of kids work in my life. The big day came; we marched and made a II. Every kid jumped up and down and yelled, they were so happy and proud of what they had accomplished. *It was great.* From then on, they believed they could do anything. And they did. That year, we made the II in marching, a II in concert, and a I in sight reading, probably the only first division the Junction band had ever made. The next school year we made Sweepstakes—a I in marching, I in sight reading, and I in concert performance—the first and only time before or since for Junction. That year, in fact, no judge gave us lower than a I at *any* competition, including the Six Flags band festival in Dallas. The band also won first place in both competition parades we entered. What a great year! We had become the standard for our region.

One fall the Junction band received an invitation to participate in the reunion activities of Paul "Bear" Bryant's first Texas A&M football team. The recent nonfiction account of that team's development, *The Junction Boys* by Jim Dent and Gene Stallings, mentions the Junction band in the last chapter. We played "dinner" music during the barbecue and stayed for the other festivities. We played the Aggie War Hymn during the ceremony. Even as a Texas Tech grad, I felt a lot of pride knowing we were a part of that great day. I actually *met* Bear Bryant.

When I left for a "better" job at the end of the 1980 season, the band boosters gave me and my family a substantial cash gift. I bought a nice wristwatch with part of the money and had it engraved "From the Junction Band Boosters." I still wear it today.

—JOHN GIBSON, *LUBBOCK*

Arts

Texas communities have always supported the arts. As soon as towns were established, opera houses opened up, and performances of Shakespeare plays began to be seen across the land. During the economic booms, especially from oil, Texans began to found art museums, symphony orchestras, opera companies, and moving picture companies (before that business went west to Hollywood). Many of the visual art collections are extensive. The Kimbell Art Museum in Fort Worth, for instance, has in its permanent collection important works by El Greco, Caravaggio, Velázquez, Mondrian, Cézanne, Picasso, and Rembrandt. Up in Canyon, the Panhandle-Plains Society's gallery contains the most comprehensive Texas art collection in the state, and also owns such treasures as the *Portrait of Anne Hogarth*, by William Hogarth, the Father of English Painting. One of my personal favorites, Georgia O'Keeffe's *Two Red Hills*, that I return to time and again, hangs in the Texas Tech Museum at Lubbock.

The great sculptor **Gutzon Borglum** and his family, who collectively chiseled Mt. Rushmore for the nation, have ties to Texas. During the 1920s they lived in San Antonizo where Gutzon completed a monument to Texas trail drivers for the grounds of the Witt Museum. Gutzon also planned a renovation of the Corpus Christi waterfront, which was never carried out. The statue of Christ that he designed for the project was completed by his son **Lincoln Borglum** (who also completed Mt. Rushmore) and placed on a mountain in South Dakota. Lincoln also sculpted the statue of **Our Lady of Loreto,** which is located in the niche above the entrance to the chapel named for her at **Presidio La Bahia.** Soldiers from this fort, located one and a half miles south of Goliad, helped the Spanish Army defend the Gulf Coast from the British during the American Revolution.

Art to Touch (Not)

The Kimball, mentioned above, often sponsors fine exhibitions, one of which I attended in order to see a small Van Gogh, *Village at Arles*. I had to stand in a long line that snaked past the pictures, which included Picassos, Cézannes, Matisses, and Monets. The crowd thought these were mighty fine, but the picture that drew gasps was the little Van Gogh. It was positioned so that you saw it suddenly as you rounded the end of a wall. It was an arrangement of thatched huts stepping down a hill, while up the hill beside them came one of Van Gogh's working peasants. The colors were like sugar candy, and the paint was impasto, quite thick. I was just approaching it when a gentleman ahead of me stepped out of line, *tapped his fingernail on the patina*, and said to his hard-of-hearing wife, "Martha, this paint's cracked!"

The guard, who wore a large identification badge on the lapel of his navy-blue blazer, appeared beside him. "Sir, please do not approach the paintings," the guard said in a low, immaculately controlled, voice.

The offender, who was nattily attired, and probably in his eighties, looked the guard up and down. Without backing up, he said, "I've been to art museums all over the world and I've never been told to stay away from the paintings. And this one's cracked. I was just telling my wife about it."

The guard explained to him that he had to move back from the painting, and once more the man explained that, in effect, if the guard was going to treat him that way, then he would take his business elsewhere, presumably to the art museums that allowed him to get cozy with their $40 million pictures. Fortunately, the man's wife came to the rescue by wandering off. She was deaf and hadn't heard any of this, and wanted to look at the Matisses around the bend.

Folk Art

Texas provides a perfect place for regular people (and a few eccentrics) to express their artistic visions. Mostly, as long as you stay inside your own yard

fence with your creations, the authorities leave you alone. If you're driving around up on the Plains, you're likely to run past a fence line exhibition of welding art—silhouettes of horses, antelopes, windmills, and cowboys—and in East Texas, maybe a yard full of wood sculpture.

Oranges, Cans, Pigs, and the OK Corral

Houston has several world-class folk art stops. The greatest is **The Orange Show**, made out of found materials, which took Jeff McKissack eleven years to build. Jeff liked oranges, so he set about building a Tribute to the Orange. He used anything that fired his imagination. You'll see wagon wheels, tractor seats, umbrellas, mosaics, mannequins, clowns, a wheeled boat, steam engines, whirligigs, ceramic tile, water fountain statues, and lots of wrought iron, all merged into an eccentric but unified layout, the same qualities all great art has. Walking through, around, and over his work, you can sense how its creator got really involved, and you can only wonder how it was that the Muse picked Jeff McKissack. Jeff opened the doors in 1979 when he was in his seventies, expecting 300,000 people a year to come visit his grand *oeuvre*. Just a few came. Disappointed, he passed away a few months later. Now Jeff's Tribute is run by the Orange Show foundation. Lots of people come to laugh and be amazed. Jeff would have been pleased.

Houston's big on this sort of thing, sporting also the **Beer Can House** (which you can imagine better than I can describe) and **Pigdom,** a bright purple shrine-to-swine house, whose owner Victoria Herberta gave up pig art when her pig was struck by lightning. I would too. Some signs you don't argue with. Last of this procession is the **OK Corral,** which is a house painted all different colors with feather dusters and whose fence is a montage of boots, guns, and pink flamingos. Take your camera. The folks back home are just not gonna believe *this*.

Bravissimo!

The Houston Grand Opera has won two Grammy Awards, one Emmy, and a Tony. Since its founding in 1955, the company has produced twenty world and six American premieres.

Late in the evening of April 13, 1958, Texan **Van Cliburn**, who became endeared to Russians as "Vanyusha," won the gold medal at the Tchaikovsky International Piano and Violin Festival in Moscow. This was during the Cold War, but that didn't prevent Russian boss Nikita Krushchev from enveloping Cliburn in a bear hug. The Russians loved him for the emotional heights he found in their beloved Tchaikovsky's *Piano Concerto No. 1 in B Flat Minor* and Rachmaninoff's *Piano Concerto No. 3, in D Minor.*

Classical Guitar Alive! hosted and produced by **Anthony Morris** from the KMFA FM radio studios in Austin, is the world's most widely appreciated radio show dedicated to the classical guitar.

Tommy Tune, the Broadway performer and director, hails from Houston.

The Fantasticks, the Broadway show, was created by composers **Tom Jones** and **Harvey Schmidt**, who received their training at the University of Texas.

Jules Bledsoe, born in Waco in 1898, sang the baritone lead in *Show Boat* on Broadway in 1927, and toured Europe and the United States as Emperor Jones in the show of that name.

Janis Joplin, who was from Port Arthur, developed her singing style in Austin, performing at Threadgill's, a converted filling station on North Lamar. Kenneth Threadgill, the proprietor, is gone from us, but the original Threadgill's still exists as a restaurant featuring fine home cooking.

Tex Ritter, actor, singer, and collector of folk songs, was born in Murvaul and went to school in Beaumont. He was the fifth inductee into the Country Music Hall of Fame and the father of John Ritter, who became popular in the role of Jack Tripper in the television series "Three's Company."

Wink's **Roy Orbison** sold more than 50 million records. Two of his memorable songs are "Oh, Pretty Woman," and "Running Scared." Elvis Presley once called Roy the world's greatest pop singer.

The great blues guitarist **Stevie Ray Vaughan** was born in Dallas in 1954, started performing in Austin in his early twenties, and by the time he died in a helicopter crash in 1990, had recorded six albums, all of which reached platinum in sales.

Amarillo native **Carolyn Jones** appeared in about thirty movies, including *Turning Point* with William Holden, *King Creole* with Elvis Presley, and *Last Train from Gun Hill* with Kirk Douglas.

Ann Sheridan, America's "Oomph Girl," was born Clara Lou Sheridan in Denton in 1915. She appeared in movies for more than thirty years. Some of her roles were in *Treasure of the Sierra Madre, The Man Who Came to Dinner*, and *King's Row*.

The first moving picture in Texas was photographed in and around Galveston after the Great Hurricane of 1900. **G.W. Bitzer** of New York's Biograph Company shot eight short takes of the aftermath.

The very first Oscar winner for Best Picture (1927), *Wings*, used army and air force bases in San Antonio for locations.

Famous Conductors

Leopold Stokowski, Sir John Barbiroli, and André Previn served tenures as conductors for the Houston Symphony Orchestra, as did Antal Dorati, Sir Georg Solti, and Kurt Masur for the Dallas Symphony Orchestra.

Texas Music(ians)

There's gotten to be so much music performed in Texas that NASA noticed from space that the state jumps around. This condition quickly became a hot news item, because legislators in surrounding states were complaining about the state lines moving, and it was complicating tax appraisals. At first, everyone thought the problem must be caused by earthquakes, so NASA assigned one of their geophysicists, Dr. Dixie Kiks, to look at the problem.

Dr. Kiks, having grown up in Lubbock, is one sharp cookie. She immediately ran a harmonic analysis on the data and determined that it came from a veritable onslaught of music being played all over the state. Because of the amount of sonic energy being generated, the earth's crust was actually on the verge of disintegrating. Texas was in danger of popping loose like a cookie and floating into the Gulf of Mexico.

This discovery was right up there with water on Mars, so NASA assembled an elite team of scientists to help Dr. Kiks study the situation in depth. NASA fitted out a Sonic Shuttle with the latest and most expensive monitoring and detection equipment. They loaded the scientists on board and blasted them into stationary orbit above Brady. This location, near the heart of Texas, would allow the crew to survey the whole state in an equitable fashion.

Within a week, the Kiks Team identified the sonic signatures of 40,000 major sound sources within the state's borders. They detected symphony orchestras or opera companies going full tilt in Houston, Dallas, Fort Worth, Abilene, Austin, El Paso, Lubbock, Amarillo, Midland-Odessa, San Antonio, and Brownsville. And there were more than 10,000 school bands playing at any one time, and thousands upon thousands of guitar players were strumming and picking. Dr. Kiks was amazed at the number of blues singers whose voices and lonesome guitars emanated from East Texas around Navasota and Marshall. Why, it seemed that out of every screen door in Grimes and Harrison Counties, there sang the ghostly reincarnation of Blind Lemon Jefferson and Leadbelly.

And the old time fiddle tunes! There was "Darling Nelly Gray" and "Sally Gooten" and "Under the Double Eagle," sailing right up out of the atmosphere, *simultaneously*, from Canyon and Marfa and Salado and Post! Turned out the fiddlers were playing the tunes to each other over their cell phones.

On one June night in 1999, the crew discovered it wasn't just Texans who were responsible for the tremors. They pinpointed the unmistakable sonic signatures of Itzhac Perlman and Luciano Pavarotti in Austin less than five blocks from one another, the first in the Bass Concert Hall and the latter in the Frank Irwin Special Events Center (that we used to be able to call the Super Drum, a term no longer politically correct).

Also in Austin, city of (it seems) a thousand clubs, cafes, and coffee houses, the electronically enhanced output from live bands was so great that it actually charged the atmosphere in the shape of a cone, and as the earth turned, this golden beacon swung outward as far as there were particles to charge, welcoming other civilizations to the venues at the Continental Club, Antone's, and Speakeasy.

As of this writing, Texans await the final report from Dr. Kiks and her crew. Legislators, pens poised, stand ready to write remedies. But symphony orchestra conductors polish their batons, opera singers trip through their arpeggios, and the fiddle players, well, they just resin up their bows. It seems that these vast, vibrating voices are just getting ready for the next hundred years.

★ ★

In 1889, **Scott Joplin,** an African American from Texarkana, published the "Maple Leaf Rag," thus inventing **ragtime** and ushering in a fad for its catchy rhythm. He didn't share in the profits from the musicians who performed it, however.

The term "blues" was first used in the 1912 song, "Dallas Blues," by Henry A. Wand. But the beginning of the blues is associated more with its patron saint, **Blind Lemon Jefferson,** who was born near Wortham in 1897.

The great Leadbelly ("The Midnight Special") was born **Huddie Ledbetter** in Louisiana and was raised in Texas, where he met Blind Lemon Jefferson. Leadbelly performed as a street minstral and saloon singer accompanying himself on the twelve-string guitar. He had been convicted of murder, then released from prison through the efforts of John A. Lomax, who, fortunately for us (and Leadbelly) was as determined a folklorist as Leadbelly was a blues man.

Bob Wills and his Texas Playboys moved Texas ranch dance music into the city, then spread it across the nation in the 1930s, '40s, and '50s. Their style was called Western Swing or Western Jazz. Some immortal songs of Bob Wills are "San Antonio Rose," "I Can't Go On This Way," "When You Leave Amarillo," "Bubbles In My Beer," "Big Balls In Cowtown" (which, in Lubbock, is known as the "Tech Stomp"), and "Faded Love." Listen to any of these and you will find a unique energy and poignancy. You may just *have* to get up and dance.

Tanya Tucker, who burst onto the country music charts in 1974 with "Delta Dawn," was born in Seminole. She received the Country Music Association's Vocalist of the Year award in 1993.

Gene Autry was born in Tioga. The breadth of his interests and the greatness of his heart were legendary. He starred in singing cowboy movies, wrote

"Rudolph the Red-Nosed Reindeer," owned the California Angels baseball team and broadcasting companies, and gave a lot of money to good causes.

John Denver ("Take Me Home, Country Roads" and "Rocky Mountain High") was born in Fort Worth, and attended Texas Tech. John appears in the 1964 Texas Tech yearbook, the *La Ventana*, with his real name, Henry Deutschendorf.

Buddy Knox, who wrote "Party Doll," was born in Happy.

Ralph Rogers, Dallas businessman and prime mover-and-shaker, helped create the **Public Broadcasting System (PBS)**.

Ernest Tubb, the Texas Troubadour, was born in Crisp, near Ennis, but he also lived in San Angelo, Anson, Fort Worth, Dallas, Midland, and Brownwood, among other famous spots. Troubadours have to move around, you know, to gather material for their songs. Apparently Mr. Tubb collected plenty, because more than one hundred of his songs made it to the country charts during the thirty or so years after 1944.

Guy Clark, one of Texas' real, true-blood song writers, was born in Rockport and grew up in Monahans. His "Desperadoes Waiting For a Train" may be the greatest metaphorical country song ever written, although most Texans try to keep literary analysis out of their country music.

Here are some Hispanic music terms. You'll need to be familiar with some of these if you listen to music in Texas, especially near the Mexican border:
- *bajo sexto* (actually 12 strings)
- *conjunto* (several instruments in a cantina—loud)
- *corrido*

- *danza*
- *despedida* (farewell)
- *enlaces* (wedding songs)
- *guitarra sexta* (six-string guitar)
- *guitarreros*
- *guitarrón*
- *os más cantadores* (the most enthusiastic singers)
- *parranda* (roaming about singing)
- *serenata* (interlude in the parranda to serenade a girl, friend, or even a parent

The *Mirador del Flor* in Corpus Christi is a pavilion and statue dedicated to the late Texas singer **Selena**. Selena was from Corpus. Jennifer Lopez plays the singer in the recent movie *Selena*.

The Houston Grand Opera's 1976 production of *Porgy and Bess* was the first to fulfill George Gershwin's intentions to perform the work as an opera and with African-American singers.

One of Texas' more historically important musical contributions was the **Stamps Quartet**, organized in 1935 by V.O. (Virgil) Stamps to help market the gospel songbooks he published. Operating out of Dallas, the original Stamps Quartet, with Stamps himself singing bass, only existed five years, but it kicked off a worldwide appreciation for religious music set to a driving, upbeat rhythm.

Artur Rubenstein at Jones Hall, 1976

When Artur Rubenstein came to Houston in 1976 to play the piano, my wife and I drove down to hear him. This was the maestro's ninetieth year, and because his vision was failing, this was to be his last solo tour. I'd heard him on

records and had seen him on late-night television, where he looked about sixty. On television he regaled his hosts with stories of the restaurants he loved around the world. He was known as quite the raconteur. But Rubenstein really was ninety years old. I thought he'd probably play a short, easy program, and that would be that. So I went more to *see* Rubenstein than to hear him.

It was a warm night, the fourth of March, and when my wife and I arrived at Jesse Jones Hall, we noticed that we didn't glitter as much as most of the crowd. To begin with, nearly everyone was dressed in coal black, men and women, and all the women wore either strands of pearls or little bitty diamonds. It was like looking into the Milky Way. The men wore their diamonds in gold lapel pins with the numbers "25" and "30" on them, designating, I suppose, the number of years they had stood in harness at one or another of Houston's oil drilling companies.

We traded our tickets for programs and walked into the hall. Our seats were centered about twenty rows from the stage. On my right, one of Houston's great doyennes of the piano-teaching business struck up a conversation. I forget her name, but before the program began, she told me about the several times she had heard Rubenstein, and then gave me a rundown on the evening's program. Although I was an orchestral French horn player, I wasn't a pianist, and I was grateful for her help.

At eight o'clock, Rubenstein walked carefully onto the stage, bowed to our applause, and went directly to the piano, where he began Beethoven's *Sonata No. 18 in E flat Major, Opus 31, No. 3.* Artur wasn't but a few phrases into the *Allegro* when the piano teacher tugged at my sleeve. "Exquisite," she whispered, "just exquisite." And it was. The combination of Beethoven and Rubenstein was hard to beat. All the nuance, tone, and spirit of complete mastery were still under his fingers, and if the piano teacher hadn't kept up her enthralled comments against my shoulder, I might not have had another analytical thought. Watching his hands bounce off the keyboard, fingers curled in the more highly articulated passages, I thought humans really did have a lot of potential that most of us weren't using if one human brain and ten fingers could keep up with all those lines, simultaneously.

Rubenstein's face, with its cloud of white hair, was something too. He had a triangular head with a very high forehead and a noble nose, and a firm, molded mouth. Within that face, as he played passages differing in passion from serenity to fury, I could detect no change. The hands did the work. Within, his face showed he was at all times sublime. Maybe that face is what you get if you play Beethoven and Chopin and Mozart five or six hours a day for eighty years.

After the Beethoven, Rubenstein played the Chopin *Sonata in B flat minor, Opus 35*, and it was, well, exquisite too. I could tell this without being a piano teacher. As far as I was concerned, Rubenstein could have been in his teens doing his first American tour. When he took his bow before intermission, my wife, who is a bassoonist, said from my left side, "Look how big his hands are."

After the formidable first half, I figured Rubenstein would show a little wear, but he came right out and played the Schumann *Carnaval,* which has a lot of different parts to it. When that was done, he gave us some preludes and a scherzo by Chopin. By now it was after ten o'clock, and Rubenstein had played and played and played. *My* physique was sagging. I noticed worn countenances around me in the pearl-and-tiny-diamond set, and my mentor-of-the-right-shoulder was noticeably calmer. But Rubenstein was unfazed. He knocked off a couple of encores and took his final bows. He seemed even more enthusiastic than when he'd started. His face was lit up. I think he was thinking, *Now I can go and reconnoiter this town.*

The Political State

A ugust, grandiose, imposing, magnificent, stately, and superb, the political
history of Texas from 1519 until 1861 has been a hard act for our modern
politicians to follow. On February 23, 1861, the people of Texas—those who
voted—took Texas out of the Union by a vote of 39,415 for secession and 13,841
against. In so doing, they turned out the last of the great founders of the
Republic of Texas, Sam Houston. As soon as the election results were in, the
other politicos called the governor in and directed him to take the oath of alle-
giance to the Confederate States of America, and Sam said something like, "No,
I don't believe I'll do that." He and his servant, Joshua, climbed up in the governor's wagon and wobbled off toward the southeast, just the two of them.
We've not seen their likes again.

Since those two departed, our politicians from the grass roots level on up
have tried to walk about in shoes of improper size. The hardest one thing any
of them ever has to do is announce what they're *for* and what they're *against*.
To come up with *issues* that anyone will pay attention to. You see, all the great

causes are over with. Opening New Lands, Gaining Independence, Setting Up a Free and Functioning Government, even Building a Great Capitol Building— all these magnificent obsessions . . . well, our forebears have already seized them by the throat, wrassled them to the ground, and finished them right up.

Our politicians are in the position Don Quixote would have been in if he'd had to build his own windmills before jousting at them. So I, for one, have terrific sympathy for these ladies and gentlemen, who, without job descriptions, have to go out and create *sturm und drang* among the folks. And let us not forget their speech writers. Trying to stir up the hunger of the masses on deadline, without a morsel in one's pen, is a formidable prospect. But, Texas being Texas, our politicians are an energetic lot, and they keep trying. When one generation wears out, there's another all shined up and ready. Some of them have been real interesting. Read on.

The Chicken Salad Case

Early in the twentieth century, the Texas Legislature got itself in a tizzy worrying over whether the governor could charge **chicken salad** to his expense account. They passed an appropriations bill specifically providing money for the governor to buy "chicken salad and punch" for the governor's mansion. This is true. *Chicken salad.* The next governor, James "Pa" Ferguson, during whose term the bill came up for signature, signed it and proceeded to practice what the legislature preached. He bought some groceries with his allowance, and some automobile tires, and some horse feed, and some gasoline. Meanwhile, the Texas Supreme Court had decided the appropriations bill was unconstitutional. While it was constitutional to use public funds to pay for utilities and ice for the mansion, groceries and other personal items weren't allowed, according to the highest court in the state.

Then the governor got into a feud with the board of regents at the University of Texas. Pa didn't like some of the faculty members, and when the

board wouldn't dismiss them, he vetoed the university's entire budget. Now, you can't have a university going around without a cent in its two thousand pockets. The fetid aroma of this squabble spread through all the fissures in the grand façades of officialdom, and soon a grand jury indicted the governor on a long list of charges. He was impeached, and stood trial before the Texas Senate. You're out of here, they told him in 1917. Furthermore, they said, you can't ever hold office in Texas again. Shoo.

A public servant with narrower stripes than Pa Ferguson wouldn't have been heard from again. But Pa kept trying to get nominated for this and that. Finally, in 1924, Pa decided to run Ma for governor. Ma—Miriam Amanda Wallace Ferguson—was his wife of twenty-five years, the mother of their two daughters. Ma and Pa's campaign slogan was brilliant: "Two governors for the price of one." Ma became the first woman to be elected governor in the United States and the second to be inaugurated. Eight years later, when the Great Depression was in full wilt, Ma again captured the governorship. She did a remarkably good job, although she incensed her opponents by pardoning a great number of prisoners. She said it cost too much during the Depression for the state to feed them. They needed to be working.

The next Texas politician I like is W. Lee "Pappy" O'Daniel, a native of Kansas, who spent most of his working life in the flour-milling business. Pappy kept getting promoted and wound up as general manager of the Burrus Mill in Fort Worth. There he gathered up a group of unknown musicians, named them the Lightcrust Doughboys, and put them on the radio. They became so popular that Pappy ran for governor using the Doughboys to get the crowds out. With another group, the Hillbilly Boys, providing entertainment for his campaign swings, he won the governorship in 1938 and 1940. Then Texans sent him to the United States Senate, where it was said that four votes were all that any of his bills ever received.

So you can see why politics keeps us enthralled. And it's a good buy. Admission to the circus is included in our taxes.

The Texas Legislature (150 House members and 31 senators) spent about $20 million to fund its five-month session that began in January and ended in May 1999. That's about a dollar for each Texan. Of course there was another $30 million or so set aside for the fiscal year to keep the utilities on between sessions and other such, you know, necessities.

A native Texan didn't serve in the United States Congress until 1891. The honor goes to **Horace Chilton.** He was born near Tyler in 1853. His father, George W., moved from Alabama in 1850, and served with the Texas Rangers and later with the Confederate Army.

Santa Anna Didn't Have a Chance

Role modeling can be a formidable force, as it was during the Texas fight for independence. When tyranny, in the person of the Napoleon of the West— General Antonio Lopez de Santa Anna—trotted across the Rio Grande into Texas, he didn't know who was arrayed against him.

At the Alamo, these were among those massacred on orders of Santa Anna:

- Andrew Jackson Harrison
- George Washington Cottle
- George Washington Cummings
- George Washington Main
- George Washington Tumlinson

At Goliad, these were among those massacred on orders of Santa Anna:

- Benjamin Franklin Burt
- George Washington Carlisle
- George Washington Daniell
- George Washington Paine
- Thomas Jefferson Dasher
- William Jefferson Merrifield

At San Jacinto, these were among those who crushed Santa Anna:

- Andrew Jackson Beard
- Andrew Jackson Berry
- Andrew Jackson Fowler
- Benjamin Franklin Bryant
- Benjamin Franklin Cage
- Benjamin Franklin Fry
- Daniel Boone Friar
- George Washington Anderson
- George Washington Browning
- George Washington Hockley
- George Washington Lang
- George Washington Petty
- George Washington Poe
- James Madison Bell
- James Monroe Hill
- Thomas Jefferson Callahan
- Thomas Jefferson Gazley, M.D.
- Thomas Jefferson Rusk
- Thomas Jefferson Sweeney

Other Texans graced with the handles of great ones:

- Abraham Lincoln Neiman (1875–1970), cofounder of Neiman-Marcus Specialty Stores
- Andrew Jackson Hamilton, governor of Texas during Reconstruction
- Andrew Jackson Houston, U.S. senator, son of Sam Houston
- Benjamin Franklin Highsmith (last man out of the Alamo alive)
- Benjamin Franklin Terry, leader of Terry's Texas Rangers during the Civil War
- Christopher Columbus Slaughter, pioneer cattleman
- George Washington Arrington, Texas Ranger
- George Washington Baines, great-grandfather of Lyndon Baines Johnson, thirty-sixth President of the U.S.
- George Washington Barnes, M.D., signed the Texas Declaration of Independence
- George Washington Brackenridge, organized San Antonio National Bank
- George Washington Littlefield, developer, town named for him
- George Washington Smyth, signed Texas Declaration of Independence
- George Washington Truett, pastor of the First Baptist Church of Dallas for forty-four years

- John Quincy Anderson (1916–75), Texas folklorist
- Thomas Jefferson Chambers, active in Texas Revolution, served as state attorney of Coahuila y Texas

While in Washington, Sam Houston whipped a representative with a hickory cane in a dispute over a contract for Indian rations. Sam was arrested and tried before the House of Representatives. He received a reprimand and had to pay a fine. His attorney was Francis Scott Key.

The Two-Bush Presidential Library: A Proposal

If our esteemed governor, George W. Bush, ever gets to be president, he'll have to find a place to build his presidential library. **Bush the First,** who was never governor, selected College Station for his, and **Johnson** (the Second, after Andrew) picked a nice oak-shaded spot in Austin near Interstate 35 for the LBJ Library. All sites in Uvalde are already taken by the ghost of **John Nance Garner,** who was FDR's vice president for two terms and nearly president himself. And of course the **Sam Rayburn** Library in Bonham (which was dedicated by former President Harry S. Truman in 1957), honors "Mr. Sam," who served forty-eight years in the U.S. Congress and who was Speaker of the House of every Democratic majority Congress between 1940 and 1961. Mr. Sam enjoyed more prestige and respect than most presidents ever receive, so it probably would not be wise, competitively speaking, to locate a new presidential library too near his home county, Fannin.

So there you are. Four prime locations, all taken. What is a president to do? As I've worked on this book, I've kept an eye out to help George the Second with this problem. The first location I'd like to recommend to him is any parcel of two acres or more above the flood plain of Two Bush Branch, a creek northwest of Fort Worth. This is pretty country, and with a well-sited façade and a billboard promising silence, the library might pull some traffic out of the two

hundred thousand deafened fans (which, incidentally, is the same number of people counted on the 1850 Census in all of Texas) who pour out of Texas Motor Speedway after race day. Two Bush Branch is about the right distance from TMS for a rest stop.

Another possibility is that if George the First would approve, George the Second could just put his library in the lobby of his dad's, you know, like you build in the garage? Maybe the Aggies at College Station could talk the folks around Two Bush Branch out of the name by trading them two birds in the hand. Then if Georges I and II wanted to build a subsidiary up at the original branch, they could call it the Two Bush Presidential Branch Branch Library. I'd go, and I know you would too.

Sam Houston's campaign trunk is displayed in the Howard-Dickenson House in Henderson. Mrs. Martha Ann Howard was Sam's cousin.

Governor Coke Stevenson's loss by 87 votes to Lyndon Baines Johnson for the U.S. Senate in 1947 was the closest race in the nation's history. The total state vote was 494,191 for Johnson and 494,104 for Stevenson, earning the future president the nickname "Landslide Lyndon."

Most interesting name of a politician: William Seat Fly (1851–1934), from Gonzales. He was a tallow factory worker, drugstore clerk, horse drover, presidential elector for Grover Cleveland in 1888, and chief justice of the Texas Supreme Court.

One of our shorter public servants was **Charles Lockhart,** who won election as state treasurer in 1930. He was about three feet nine inches tall. Before winning that election, he served as sergeant-at-arms for the Texas Legislature. About the same time, a newspaper anointed 400-pound W. W. Early of Hermleigh with the sobriquet "Largest Mayor of the Smallest Town."

All Hot Air Does Not Rise

When he got up to speak at a political rally, **Texan James Harvey Davis** just blew his opponents away, like a cyclone. Cyclone Davis campaigned for Woodrow Wilson in 1912 and was elected to the U.S. Congress in 1914, where he became known for his stance in favor of agricultural reform. When World War I came along, he introduced an eyebrow-raising bill. Cyclone proposed that the nation draft more than bodies. He thought we ought to draft rich people's money. Cyclone lost his bid for reelection in 1916. It wasn't until sixteen years later that he legally changed his name to James Harvey Cyclone Davis.

Texas was the only state in the Confederacy to put the **question of secession** to a vote of its citizens.

Sam Houston, former president, governor, and senator of Texas, was against withdrawing Texas from the Union. Too much work had gone into getting *in*. Besides, he said, there wasn't any way the South could win a war with the North. According to Sam's servant Joshua, President Lincoln offered Sam the federal navy to keep him in office. Houston took a vote of his friends, and they advised him to decline Lincoln's offer. He followed their advice, then withdrew from politics. He died during the Civil War at his home in Huntsville.

Texas is the only state that permits residents to cast absentee ballots from space. The first person to exercise this right to vote while in orbit was astronaut David Wolf, who cast his vote for Houston mayor via e-mail from the Russian space station *Mir* in November 1997. This was the *highest* voter participation in history.

The Texan's Bill of Rights

Declaration

We, the people of the State of Texas, in order to preserve happiness, foster international understanding, and secure our future welfare do hereby resolve, declare, and decree that certain inherent and inalienable rights are reserved for every citizen of the Lone Star State. Furthermore, these solemn duties, when performed by one or more True Texans should receive encouragement of all civil authorities and protection of the military whether at home or abroad.

Articles

Texans, at their sole discretion, may:

1st Use "fixin' to" as a prefix for anything about to transpire. As in "Looks like it's fixin' to come a blue norther." Describe a location as "over yonder" and expect you to know where it is.

2nd When asked where we're from while traveling abroad, say "Texas."

3rd Use "a tall" instead of "at all." As in "You haven't been listening to me a tall, have you?"

4th Wear our hats and boots in places like Paris, France, even though we may not wear them at home.

5th Own six dozen gimme caps so we'll have enough.

6th After waiting out a long drouth, buy a new pickup truck as the first item of business, before groceries.

7th Use "'sta bien" for "good," "shore" for "sure," and "'at's awright" for "that's okay."

8th Drive ten hours from the Panhandle to the Gulf of Mexico to drop a hook in salt water before dark.

9th   Build a fine storm cellar, then when tornado season arrives, fill it up with canned goods and watch the lightning strikes from our front window.

10th   Drive a hundred miles or so between quitting time and midnight just to buy a Christmas present or a load of groceries, or take a friend a vest we just finished quilting.

11th   Think other American citizens odd for not being raised on okra, jalapeños, chicken-fried steak, and tamales.

12th   Use "little lady" to greet any female who looks as if she deserves respect, and mean no offense.

13th   Turn highbrow into lowbrow at the drop of a hat.

14th   Build a tall building in a single bound.

15th   Loan you our posthole diggers, then show up to help build fence though you never asked us.

16th   Run up our phone bills reminding friends and relatives to eat their black-eyed peas on New Year's Day.

17th   Play Dominoes and Forty-Two 'til the cows come home.

Sources

Author's note: Of valuable use throughout all sections were *The Handbook of Texas Online* (http://www.tsha.utexas.edu/handbook/online/index.html), a joint project of The General Libraries at the University of Texas at Austin and the Texas State Historical Association; *The Texas Almanac 2000,* published by *The Dallas Morning News;* and the various printed editions of *The Handbook of Texas*, published by the Texas Historical Commission.

Where We Came From
Imperial Texas, An Interpretive Essay in Cultural Geography, D.W. Meinig, University of Texas Press, 1975; *The Mexican Frontier, 1821–1846,* David J. Weber, University of New Mexico Press, 1982; *Old Texas Trails,* J.W. Williams, Eakin Press, 1979; *Texas: The Beginning, 1519–1834,* Ed Syers, Texian Press, 1978; *A Texas-Mexican Cancionero, Folksongs of the Lower Border,* Américo Paredes, University of Illinois Press, 1976; *Stephen F. Austin, Empresario of Texas*, Gregg Cantrell, Yale University Press, 1999; *Juneteenth Texas*, ed. Francis E. Abernathy et al., University of North Texas Press; *The Texas Courthouse*, June Rayfield Welch and J. Larry Nance, Texian Press, 1971; *The Centennial Book*, ed. Patrice McKinney, Mitchell County Centennial, Inc., 1981; *Czech Texans,* Institute of Texan Cultures, n.d.; collection of Edward Larocque Tinker in the Texas Memorial Museum; *Los Mesteños, Spanish Ranching in Texas 1721–1821*, Jack Jackson, Texas A&M University Press, n.d.

Where We Live
Lovingly, Georgia, The Complete Correspondence of Georgia O'Keeffe and Anita Pollitzer, ed. Clive Giboire, Simon and Schuster/Touchstone, 1990, p. 183; *The Texas Courthouse*, June Rayfield Welch and J. Larry Nance, Texian Press, 1971; *Texas Architect,* May–June 1986, pp. 78–87; *Rusk County Chamber of Commerce Tourist Information*, Henderson, TX; *Town Planning in Frontier America*, John Reps, University of Missouri Press, 1980; Texas Historical Commission Records, Job #3315: Irion County Historical Marker 1970, THC Library, Austin; *The Centennial Book*, ed. Patrice McKinney, Mitchell County Centennial, Inc., 1981, p. 7; *Texas Atlas and Gazetteer*, Delorme Mapping, 1995; *Texas Department of Transportation Official Highway Map, 1999; Dallas Morning News,* 18 April, 8 May, 1999; *Tapadero: The Making of a Cowboy*, Willie Newbury Lewis, University of Texas Press, 1972; *Red River Women*, Sherrie S. McLeRoy, Republic of Texas Press, 1996; *My Frontier Days and Indian Fights on the Plains of Texas*, Captain Henry W. Strong, n.p., n.d.; *Pioneer Profiles*, Jean Littlepage Everett, 1998, p. 115; *Roadside Geology*

of Texas, Darwin Spearing, Mountain Press Publishing Company, 1998; *Texas Myths*, ed. Robert F. O'Conner, Texas A&M University Press, 1986; Texas Water Development Board Web site; *USA Today*, 30 Aug., 1999; *Austin American Statesman*, 6 and 27 June, 12 Aug., 5 Sept., 1999, 3, 9 Jan., 30 Aug., 2000; *Mason and Mason County*, Stella Gipson Polk, Nortex Press, 1980, pp. 37, 41; *The Wind*, Dorothy Scarborough, University of Texas Press, 1979; *Texas Atlas and Gazetteer*, Delorme Mapping, Yarmouth, Maine, 1995; *Texas Almanac 1947–1948, Dallas Morning News*, 1946, p. 287; *Texas Almanac 2000–2001, Dallas Morning News*, 1999, p. 555;*Those Buried Texans*, Tom Allen, Hendrick-Long Publishing Co., 1980; *Microsoft Streets and Trips 2000* CD Rom 1999; *Southern Living*, Sept. 1966; *Nameless Towns, Texas Sawmill Communities, 1880–1942*, Thad Sitton and James H. Conrad, University of Texas Press, 1998.

Our Work Ethic

Snyder Scrapbook, Hidetown to Boom Town, Aline Parks, Walsworth Publishing Co., 1998; Texas Department of Economic Development; *Handbook of Texas Online; Rusk County Chamber of Commerce Tourist Information*, Henderson, TX; *Lubbock Avalanche-Journal; West Texas Historical Association Yearbook*, October 1962, p. 62; *Roadside Geology of Texas*, Darwin Spearing, Mountain Press Publishing Company, 1998, pp. 53–57; *Stephen F. Austin, Empresario of Texas*, Gregg Cantrell, Yale University Press, 1999; *Mirrors, Mice, and Moustaches, A Sampling of Superstitions & Popular Beliefs in Texas*, George D. Hendricks, Texas Folklore Society, 1966; *Those Buried Texans*; *Snyder Signal*, Snyder, TX., 13 Mar. 1914.

Texas Cuisine

Austin American Statesman, 28 June, 19 Sept. 1999; *Soldiers and Settlers, Military Supply in the Southwest*, Darlis A. Miller, University of New Mexico Press, 1989; *Searchlight Recipe Book*, Copper Publications, Inc., 1946; *A Journey through Texas*, Frederick Law Olmsted, 1857, *Austin Chronicle*, 16 July 1999, p. 44; Texas State Aquarium, Monica K. De La Garza, P.R. Director, via e-mail 12 July 2000.

How We Have Fun

Austin American Statesman, 7, 11, 25 July, 19, 25 Sept., 25 Nov. 1999; literature of the Texas Travel Industry Association; *Grasses of Texas*, Frank W. Gould, Texas A&M University Press, 1975, p. 1; *Texas Coastal Bend*, Alpha Kennedy Wood, n.p., 1979, p. 84.

Education and the Arts

Snapshot 1997–98, Texas Education Agency; "Ambassador from Texas," *Encyclopedia Year Book, 1959*, the Grolier Society, page 108. *Daily Texan*, University of Texas, 4 Oct.

1999; *Smithville Times,* 27 May 1999; *Smithville Independent School District Web Page, Austin American Statesman,* 18 Oct. 1999, 1 Jan. Sec. C p. 4, 19 March, 2000; *Texas from Spindletop to World War II,* James L. Haley, St. Martin's Press, 1993, p. 21; *A Texas-Mexican Cancionero,* Américo Paredes, University of Illinois Press, 1976, p. xxiv.

The Political State

Handbook of Texas Online; Those Buried Texans, Tom Allen, Hendrick-Long Publishing Co., 1980; *Texas Coastal Bend,* Alpha Kennedy Wood, no pub. 1980; *The Government and Politics of Texas,* Clifton McCleskey, 1966.

About the Author

Wells Teague was born in Littlefield, on the South Plains of Texas, where his parents farmed 160 acres of fine sandy loam. He went to school at Sweetwater, Austin, and Lubbock, then attended Texas Tech University, where he was a student of the noted French horn player Anthony Brittin. Teague was drum major of the Goin' Band From Raiderland for four years. During his college years he could do a running goose step for one hundred yards while wearing a two-foot-high rabbit-fur shako and carrying a chrome-plated baton. He says this was highly desirable to do if you got the chance, on the South Plains of Texas in the Sixties.

Teague began writing fiction while an undergraduate, and after a stint directing bands at Rankin, Texas, he attended the Writers Workshop at the University of Iowa. Here he studied with Richard Yates, Vance Bourjaily, and the great southern humorist, William Price Fox. During those years, Teague published pieces in *audience, fiction international, Texas Monthly, Triquarterly, Chicago Review,* and *Texas Parade.* Later, he published a juvenile novel about the Texas Indian Wars, *Theo the Indian Fighter.*[1] He has worked for the Texas Education Agency as a technology planner, writer, and editor. He says that writing *Calling Texas Home* is the most fun he's had in years. Wells Teague lives in Austin.

[1] *Theo The Indian Fighter,* Eakin Press, 1987, ISBN 0-89015-614-X, juvenile novel about the frontier Indian wars of the 1870s; used as resource in 4th grade Texas history.

About the Press

Wildcat Canyon Press publishes books that embrace such subjects as friendship, spirituality, women's issues, and home and family, all with a focus on self-help and personal growth. Great care is taken to create books that inspire reflection and improve the quality of our lives. Our books invite sharing and are frequently given as gifts.

For a catalog of our publications, please write:

Wildcat Canyon Press
2716 Ninth Street
Berkeley, California 94710
Phone: (510) 848-3600
Fax: (510) 848-1326
Visit our website at www.wildcatcanyon.com

★ ★

More Wildcat Canyon Titles

LIFE AFTER BABY: FROM PROFESSIONAL WOMAN TO BEGINNER PARENT
An emotional compass for career women navigating the unfamiliar seas of parenthood.
Wynn McClenahan Burkett
$14.95 ISBN 1-885171-44-7

STEPMOTHERS & STEPDAUGHTERS: RELATIONSHIPS OF CHANCE, FRIENDSHIPS FOR A LIFETIME
True stories and commentary that look at the relationship between stepmother and stepdaughter as strong, loving, and a lifelong union.
Karen L. Annarino
$14.95 ISBN 1-885171-46-3

BOUNTIFUL WOMEN: LARGE WOMEN'S SECRETS FOR LIVING THE LIFE THEY DESIRE
The definitive book for women who believe that "bountiful" is a way of being in this world, not a particular size.
Bonnie Bernell
$14.95 ISBN 1-885171-47-1

AND WHAT DO YOU DO? WHEN WOMEN CHOOSE TO STAY HOME
At last, a book for the 7.72 million women who don't work outside the home—by choice!
Loretta Kaufman and Mary Quigley
$14.95 ISBN 1-885171-40-4

40 OVER 40: 40 THINGS EVERY WOMAN OVER 40 NEEDS TO KNOW ABOUT GETTING DRESSED
An image consultant shows women over forty how to love what they wear and wear what they love.
Brenda Kinsel
$16.95 ISBN 1-885171-42-0

★ ★

GUESS WHO'S COMING TO DINNER: CELEBRATING CROSS-CULTURAL, INTERFAITH, AND INTERRACIAL RELATIONSHIPS
True-life tales of the deep bonds that diversity makes.
Brenda Lane Richardson
$13.95 ISBN 1-885171-41-2

OUT OF THE BLUE: ONE WOMAN'S STORY OF STROKE, LOVE, AND SURVIVAL
A must read for stroke survivors and their families.
Bonnie Sherr Klein
$14.95 ISBN 1-885171-45-5

STILL FRIENDS: LIVING HAPPILY EVER AFTER…EVEN IF YOUR MARRIAGE FALLS APART
True stories of couples who have managed to keep their friendships intact after splitting up.
Barbara Quick
$12.95 ISBN 1-885171-36-6

CALLING CALIFORNIA HOME: A LIVELY LOOK AT WHAT IT MEANS TO BE A CALIFORNIAN
A cornucopia of facts and trivia about Californians and the California Spirit.
Heather Waite
$14.95 ISBN 1-885171-37-4

CALLING THE MIDWEST HOME: A LIVELY LOOK AT THE ORIGINS, ATTITUDES, QUIRKS, AND CURIOSITIES OF AMERICA'S HEARTLANDERS
A loving look at the people who call the Midwest home—whether they live there or not.
Carolyn Lieberg
$14.95 ISBN 1-885171-12-9

BREASTS: OUR MOST PUBLIC PRIVATE PARTS
One hundred and one women reveal the naked truth about breasts.
Meema Spadola
$13.95 ISBN 1-885171-27-7

I Was My Mother's Bridesmaid: Young Adults Talk About Thriving in a Blended Family
The truth about growing up in a "combined family."
Erica Carlisle and Vanessa Carlisle
$13.95 ISBN 1-885171-34-X

The Courage to Be a Stepmom: Finding Your Place Without Losing Yourself
Hands-on advice and emotional support for stepmothers.
Sue Patton Thoele
$14.95 ISBN 1-885171-28-5

Celebrating Family: Our Lifelong Bonds with Parents and Siblings
True stories about how baby boomers have recognized the flaws of their families and come to love them as they are.
Lisa Braver Moss
$13.95 ISBN 1-885171-30-7

Aunties: Our Older, Cooler, Wiser Friends
An affectionate tribute to the unique and wonderful women we call "Auntie."
Tamara Traeder and Julienne Bennett
$12.95 ISBN 1-885171-22-6

The Aunties Keepsake Book: The Story of Our Friendship
A beautiful way to tell the wonderful story of you and your auntie or niece.
Tamara Traeder and Julienne Bennett
$19.95 ISBN 1-885171-29-3

Little Sisters: The Last But Not The Least
A feisty look at the trials and tribulations, joys and advantages of being a little sister.
Carolyn Lieberg
$13.95 ISBN 1-885171-24-2

girlfriends: INVISIBLE BONDS, ENDURING TIES
Filled with true stories of ordinary women and extraordinary friendships, *girlfriends* has become a gift of love among women everywhere.
Carmen Renee Berry and Tamara Traeder
$12.95 ISBN 1-885171-08-0
Also Available: Hardcover gift edition, $20.00 ISBN 1-885171-20-X

girlfriends TALK ABOUT MEN: SHARING SECRETS FOR A GREAT RELATIONSHIP
This book shares insights from real women in real relationships—not just from the "experts."
Carmen Renee Berry and Tamara Traeder
$14.95 ISBN 1-885171-21-8

girlfriends FOR LIFE: FRIENDSHIPS WORTH KEEPING FOREVER
This follow-up to the best-selling *girlfriends* is an all-new collection of stories and anecdotes about the amazing bonds of women's friendships.
Carmen Renee Berry and Tamara Traeder
$13.95 ISBN 1-885171-32-3

A girlfriends GIFT: REFLECTIONS ON THE EXTRAORDINARY BONDS OF FRIENDSHIP
A lively collection of hundreds of quotations from the *girlfriends* books series.
Carmen Renee Berry and Tamara Traeder
$15.95 ISBN 1-885171-43-9

A COUPLE OF FRIENDS: THE REMARKABLE FRIENDSHIP BETWEEN STRAIGHT WOMEN AND GAY MEN
What makes the friendships between straight women and gay men so wonderful? Find out in this honest and fascinating book.
Robert H. Hopcke and Laura Rafaty
$14.95 ISBN 1-885171-33-1

INDEPENDENT WOMEN: CREATING OUR LIVES, LIVING OUR VISIONS
How women value independence and relationship and are redefining their lives to accommodate both.
Debra Sands Miller
$16.95 ISBN 1-885171-25-0

THOSE WHO CAN…COACH! CELEBRATING COACHES WHO MAKE A DIFFERENCE
Inspirational stories from men and women who remember a coach who made a
lasting difference in their lives.
Lorraine Glennon and Roy Leavitt
$12.95 ISBN 1-885171-49-8

THOSE WHO CAN…TEACH! CELEBRATING TEACHERS WHO MAKE A DIFFERENCE
A tribute to our nation's teachers.
Lorraine Glennon and Mary Mohler
$12.95 ISBN 1-885171-35-8

LIVING WITH DOGS: TALES OF LOVE, COMMITMENT & ENDURING FRIENDSHIP
A tribute to our unique friendship with dogs—a great gift for any "dog person."
Henry and Mary Ellen Korman
$13.95 ISBN 1-885171-19-6

THE WORRYWART'S COMPANION: TWENTY-ONE WAYS TO SOOTHE YOURSELF AND WORRY
SMART
The perfect gift for anyone who lies awake at night worrying.
Dr. Beverly Potter
$11.95 ISBN 1-885171-15-3

DIAMONDS OF THE NIGHT: THE SEARCH FOR SPIRIT IN YOUR DREAMS
Combines the story of "Annie" with a therapist's wisdom about the power of
dreams.
James Hagan, Ph.D.
$16.95 ISBN 1-879290-12-X

Books are available at fine retailers nationwide.

Prices subject to change without notice.